AI Toolb

Empowering the Learner

Book Two of the NewBits AI Trilogy

*Our Journey Continues as We Venture into the
Rich Tapestry of Artificial Intelligence Solutions.*

*Through Models, Tools, and Platforms, We Will Be
Exploring Language, Data, Audio/Vision,
Healthcare, Robotics, and Gaming Applications,
Empowering You to Transform Ideas into Reality.*

"It's all about the bits…especially the new bits."

GIL OREN

GIL OREN

AI TOOLBOX: EMPOWERING THE LEARNER

AI Toolbox: Empowering the Learner
Book Two of the NewBits AI Trilogy
by Gil Oren

Published by NewBits Media
A Division of NewBits, LLC
newbits.ai
First Edition: 2024
Printed in the United States of America

ISBN: 9798300471453

This is a work of non-fiction. All information presented is believed to be accurate at the time of publication. The author and publisher disclaim any liability in connection with the use of this information.

AI DISCLOSURE
This book was created in collaboration with artificial intelligence. Content was partially generated, edited, and refined using leading AI language models. The author has carefully reviewed, verified, and takes full responsibility for all content. This approach aligns with our mission at NewBits Media, a division of NewBits, LLC, to demonstrate practical applications of AI technology while maintaining high standards of quality and accuracy.

Cover design created with AI assistance.

Some names and identifying details may have been changed to protect the privacy of individuals.

GIL OREN

For Frieda and Yair "Jerry" Oren, and

Sharon and Jerry "Dr. J." Goodwin

- whose wisdom, love, unwavering support, and guiding principles have shaped our family's journey and inspired generations.

GIL OREN

TABLE OF CONTENTS

Welcome to the NewBits AI Trilogy: Book Two......................9

Chapter 1: Introduction to AI Toolbox...............................13

Chapter 2: Models, Tools, and Platforms Explained.............33

Chapter 3: Open Source vs Proprietary AI.............................49

Chapter 4: Language AI Solutions 73

Chapter 5: Data AI Solutions..99

Chapter 6: Audio/Vision AI Solutions 123

Chapter 7: Healthcare AI Solutions......................................147

Chapter 8: Robotics AI Solutions 171

Chapter 9: Gaming AI solutions 195

Chapter 10: Cross-Domain AI Projects.................................219

Chapter 11: AI Development Challenges 245

Preview of Book Three, *AI Frontier: Navigating the Cutting Edge* 271

AI Glossary: Bit by Bit..273

About newbits.ai 291

Our Name: newbits.ai 295

Extended Dedications 299

About the Author..301

GIL OREN

WELCOME TO THE NEWBITS AI TRILOGY:
BOOK TWO

Having laid the foundation of AI understanding in Book One, we now stand at an exciting threshold. The fundamentals we explored, from basic principles to ethical considerations, have prepared us for this next crucial step: putting AI to work. As the technological landscape continues to evolve at an unprecedented pace, the ability to effectively leverage AI tools and solutions has become increasingly crucial for success in virtually every field.

AI Toolbox: Empowering the Learner transforms knowledge into capability. Where Book One illuminated AI's nature, this volume reveals its practical power through the rich ecosystem of solutions available today. We'll explore the landscape of AI models, tools, and platforms that are reshaping industries and enabling innovation across domains. This practical knowledge has become essential not just for technologists, but for professionals across all sectors seeking to enhance their capabilities and drive innovation.

Our journey now takes us deep into practical applications,

from language and data analytics to healthcare and gaming. You'll discover how different AI solutions address real-world challenges, learn to evaluate their capabilities, and understand how to leverage them effectively. Whether you're a professional looking to implement AI solutions or an enthusiast eager to explore AI's potential, this book provides the practical knowledge you need to navigate this dynamic landscape.

The timing of this volume couldn't be more crucial. As AI solutions become increasingly accessible, the gap between their availability and effective utilization continues to widen. Organizations and individuals often find themselves overwhelmed by the sheer variety of options available, struggling to identify which tools best suit their needs. This book bridges that gap, providing clear guidance through the complex ecosystem of AI solutions.

This practical exploration represents the crucial middle chapter of our trilogy. Building on the fundamentals from Book One, it prepares you for the cutting-edge developments we'll explore in Book Three, *AI Frontier: Navigating the Cutting Edge*. Each chapter adds another tool to your AI toolkit, empowering you to move from understanding to implementation. The knowledge gained here will serve as a springboard for exploring future innovations and advancements in AI technology.

Throughout this book, we maintain our commitment to accessibility and practical application. Complex concepts are broken down into manageable components, with real-world examples illustrating how various AI solutions can be effectively implemented. You'll gain not just knowledge of available tools, but the understanding needed to evaluate and select the right solutions for specific challenges.

The practical skills developed through this volume will prove invaluable in an increasingly AI-driven world. As organizations across all sectors incorporate AI solutions into their operations, the ability to understand and effectively utilize these tools becomes a crucial differentiator. Whether you're looking to enhance business processes, drive innovation, or simply explore the possibilities AI offers, this book provides the practical foundation you need.

The path ahead is both practical and inspiring. Through real-world examples and clear explanations, we'll demystify the tools that are making AI accessible to everyone. We'll explore how different sectors are leveraging AI solutions to transform their operations, and how individuals are using these tools to enhance their capabilities and achieve their goals.

Let's continue our journey together, transforming knowledge into capability and ideas into reality. Welcome to the next phase of your AI journey, where understanding meets application, and potential becomes achievement.

CHAPTER 1: INTRODUCTION TO AI TOOLBOX

Picture yourself in 2015, when implementing AI required deep expertise in machine learning, substantial computing resources, and complex infrastructure. Organizations needed specialized teams, extensive development time, and significant investment to build even basic AI applications. Today, that same capability might require just a few lines of code and an API (Application Programming Interface) key.

This transformation marks a fundamental shift in how we access and implement artificial intelligence. The emergence of cloud-based AI services, open-source frameworks, and pre-trained models has revolutionized the accessibility of AI technology. What once required custom development can now be accomplished through readily available solutions.

The journey to this accessibility follows a fascinating progression. In the early 2010s, implementing AI meant building almost everything from scratch. Organizations needed expertise in machine learning algorithms, substantial computational resources, and the ability to gather and process massive datasets. Few companies outside major tech firms could afford such investments, limiting AI's practical applications.

Consider the evolution of natural language processing. In 2018, building a sophisticated language model required massive datasets, specialized expertise, and months of training time. The release of pre-trained models and APIs has since enabled developers to implement advanced language capabilities within their applications in hours rather than months. This progression from complex development to accessible implementation represents a core theme in AI's recent evolution.

The introduction of cloud-based AI services by major technology companies has played a crucial role in this transformation. These services provide APIs for common AI tasks like image recognition, text analysis, and speech processing. Developers can now integrate these capabilities into their applications without managing the underlying infrastructure or training their own models.

This democratization gained momentum through several key developments. Cloud computing made computational resources accessible on demand. Pre-trained models eliminated the need to build everything from scratch. Development frameworks simplified the implementation process. Each advancement removed barriers to entry, making AI increasingly practical for organizations of all sizes.

Open-source AI frameworks have similarly transformed the development landscape. TensorFlow's release in 2015, followed by PyTorch in 2016, made sophisticated machine learning tools freely available to developers worldwide. These frameworks, combined with pre-trained models and documented implementations, have significantly lowered the barriers to AI development.

The emergence of AI solutions marketplaces represents another crucial step in this evolution. These platforms offer pre-built solutions for common needs, allowing organizations to implement AI capabilities without extensive development effort. This "solutions first" approach shifts focus from technical complexity to practical application, enabling faster implementation and innovation.

This democratization extends beyond development tools to complete solutions. Today's AI marketplace offers pre-built solutions for specific business needs, from customer service automation to predictive maintenance systems. These solutions package sophisticated AI capabilities in forms that organizations can implement without extensive AI expertise.

The healthcare sector illustrates this evolution clearly. Medical imaging analysis, once requiring custom AI development, now has available pre-trained models and specialized healthcare AI solutions. These tools allow healthcare providers to implement AI capabilities within their existing workflows, focusing on application rather than development.

In scientific research, cloud computing platforms now offer specialized AI tools for data analysis, enabling researchers to apply machine learning techniques without becoming AI specialists. This accessibility has accelerated research across fields, from genomics to climate science.

Creative industries have experienced similar transformation. Artists and designers now access AI tools for image generation and manipulation, while musicians have AI-assisted composition tools. These solutions demonstrate how accessible AI has become across diverse domains.

The business landscape particularly reflects this evolution. Small companies can now implement AI capabilities that were once exclusive to large corporations. From predictive analytics to automated document processing, sophisticated AI solutions have become accessible across organization sizes and industries.

This evolution continues as new models and tools emerge. Large language models, computer vision systems, and specialized AI solutions become increasingly refined and accessible. Yet this progress brings both opportunities and responsibilities, the need to understand these tools' capabilities, limitations, and appropriate applications.

Building upon the foundational knowledge established in Book One, we now stand ready to explore the practical implementation of AI solutions. Understanding both what these solutions can do and how to implement them effectively becomes crucial for success in today's AI-enhanced world.

As we venture deeper into this AI toolbox, understanding its core components becomes essential. How do models, tools, and platforms work together to create powerful AI solutions? What options are available for different needs and applications? Understanding these fundamental building blocks will illuminate the practical AI solutions transforming our world today.

Having traced the evolution of AI accessibility, let's examine the fundamental components that make up today's AI toolbox. Understanding these building blocks provides the foundation for exploring specific solutions throughout our journey.

At the core of every AI solution are models, trained systems designed to perform specific tasks. Models represent the computational engines of AI solutions, processing inputs and generating outputs based on patterns learned during training. Like the neural networks we explored in Book One, these models form the foundation of AI capabilities. Each model serves a specific purpose, whether processing language, analyzing images, or making predictions from data.

The capabilities of AI models stem from their training data and architecture. A model designed for language processing learns from text examples, while a computer vision model learns from images. This specialization allows models to excel at specific tasks while requiring careful matching of model capabilities to intended applications. Understanding model characteristics helps guide selection and implementation decisions.

Model implementation has evolved significantly. Early AI

required organizations to build and train their own models from scratch, a resource-intensive process requiring substantial expertise. Today, pre-trained models offer sophisticated capabilities ready for implementation. These pre-trained models can often be fine-tuned for specific needs, combining the benefits of established capabilities with customization potential.

The model ecosystem continues to expand through research and development. New architectures emerge, offering improved capabilities or efficiency. Training techniques advance, enabling better performance or requiring less data. Understanding these developments helps organizations track potential improvements to their AI implementations.

Tools form the next essential layer, providing the software and utilities needed to work with AI models. Development frameworks help create and modify models. Testing utilities verify model performance. Deployment tools help move models into production environments. Together, these tools enable the practical implementation of AI capabilities.

The tool landscape reflects the maturing AI industry. Early tools required significant technical expertise and offered limited automation. Modern tools provide more accessible interfaces, automated processes, and integrated development environments. This evolution has made AI implementation more practical for a broader range of organizations.

The tool ecosystem continues to evolve, with new utilities emerging to address specific needs. Some tools focus on data preparation, helping organize and clean the information models need to learn. Others specialize in model optimization, ensuring efficient operation in real-world conditions. Still others handle monitoring and maintenance, helping maintain solution performance over time.

Tool selection significantly influences implementation success. Different tools offer varying levels of automation, customization options, and integration capabilities.

Understanding these differences helps organizations choose tools that match their technical capabilities and implementation needs.

Platforms complete our component trinity, providing the environments where models and tools come together. Development platforms offer spaces to build and test solutions, while deployment platforms manage operational implementation. Each platform type serves distinct purposes in the AI implementation process.

Modern AI platforms handle crucial operational tasks automatically. They manage computational resources, scale solutions based on demand, and monitor performance. This automation reduces the technical complexity of implementing AI solutions, allowing organizations to focus on practical applications rather than infrastructure management.

Platform capabilities vary significantly. Some focus on specific types of AI solutions, offering optimized environments for particular applications. Others provide general-purpose infrastructure suitable for diverse implementations. Understanding these differences helps guide platform selection based on specific needs.

The integration of these components creates functional AI solutions. Models provide the processing capabilities, tools enable practical work with those capabilities, and platforms ensure reliable operation. Understanding how these components work together helps guide effective solution implementation.

Consider the relationship between components in practical implementation. A platform might provide the computational resources needed to run a model, while tools help optimize that model's performance for specific use cases. This interplay between components determines both capabilities and limitations of AI solutions.

Component selection significantly influences implementation success. The right combination of model, tools, and platform creates efficient, effective solutions.

Mismatched components can lead to technical challenges or limited functionality. Understanding these relationships helps guide component selection for specific needs.

The modular nature of modern AI solutions offers important advantages. Organizations can choose components that match their specific requirements, replacing or upgrading individual elements as needs evolve. This flexibility helps create sustainable, adaptable solutions while managing implementation complexity.

As we explore specific AI solutions throughout this book, we'll see how these components combine in different ways to address various needs. This foundational understanding of components illuminates the practical possibilities of AI implementation, guiding effective solution development and deployment.

Moving from understanding AI to implementing AI solutions requires a fundamental shift in perspective. While Book One established the theoretical foundations of artificial intelligence, successful implementation demands a practical, solution-focused mindset. This transition marks the beginning of our journey from knowledge to capability.

This transition begins with recognizing the difference between understanding AI capabilities and applying them effectively. Knowledge of how neural networks function or how machine learning works provides crucial context, but implementation requires focusing on specific problems and their solutions. This practical orientation helps guide effective decision-making throughout the implementation process.

The implementation mindset starts with clear problem definition. Rather than asking what AI can do, successful implementers ask what specific challenges they need to solve. This problem-first approach helps identify appropriate solutions while avoiding the common pitfall of implementing technology for its own sake. Understanding the true nature of a challenge often reveals simpler or more effective solutions than initially considered.

Successful implementers recognize the importance of starting small and scaling gradually. Beginning with manageable projects allows organizations to build experience and confidence while minimizing risks. This approach helps develop internal expertise while demonstrating value through early successes. As capabilities grow, organizations can tackle increasingly complex implementations.

Understanding the practical constraints of real-world implementation proves equally important. Every implementation operates within specific limitations of time, resources, and capabilities. Successful implementation requires balancing ideal solutions with practical realities, making informed compromises while maintaining focus on core objectives. These constraints often drive innovation, leading to creative solutions that maximize available resources.

Solution types vary significantly in their implementation requirements. Some solutions work essentially out of the box, requiring minimal customization. Others need substantial adaptation to specific needs. Still others must be built largely from scratch. Understanding these differences helps set realistic expectations and guide implementation planning. Each type brings its own advantages and challenges that must be considered during solution selection.

The choice between open source and proprietary solutions represents another key consideration. Open source solutions offer flexibility and transparency, often with active development communities providing support and improvements. Proprietary solutions typically offer more polished implementations with professional support, though sometimes with less flexibility. Each approach brings distinct advantages and limitations that must be weighed against specific needs.

Implementation success requires ongoing learning and adaptation. AI solutions continue to evolve, offering new capabilities and approaches. Maintaining awareness of these developments while focusing on practical application helps organizations leverage new opportunities effectively. This balance between stability and innovation helps create sustainable implementations.

The implementation mindset emphasizes practical testing and validation. Successful implementers develop clear metrics for success, test solutions thoroughly before deployment, and monitor performance continuously. This empirical approach helps ensure solutions deliver real value while identifying areas for improvement.

Risk assessment takes on particular importance in implementation planning. Every AI solution has limitations and potential failure modes. Successful implementers maintain realistic expectations while building appropriate safeguards and fallback mechanisms into their solutions. Understanding and planning for potential risks helps create robust implementations.

Resource planning takes on particular importance in implementation. Beyond immediate development or procurement costs, organizations must consider ongoing operational requirements, maintenance needs, and potential scaling costs. This comprehensive view of resource requirements helps ensure sustainable implementation. Successful planning accounts for both current needs and future growth.

Stakeholder engagement proves crucial for implementation success. AI solutions often affect multiple parts of an organization, requiring buy-in and support from various groups. Understanding and addressing stakeholder concerns helps create successful implementations while ensuring solutions meet real organizational needs.

Documentation and knowledge sharing support long-term success. Recording implementation decisions, challenges encountered, and lessons learned helps organizations build institutional knowledge. This documentation supports both current operations and future implementations while enabling effective knowledge transfer.

Perhaps most importantly, the implementation mindset recognizes that success often comes through iteration. Initial implementations may meet basic needs while leaving room for improvement. This iterative approach allows organizations to build experience with AI solutions while progressively enhancing their capabilities. Each iteration brings new insights and opportunities for enhancement.

The implementation mindset also encompasses understanding the broader impact of AI solutions. Beyond technical considerations, successful implementers consider how solutions affect workflows, user experiences, and organizational processes. This holistic view helps create implementations that deliver real value while supporting positive change.

As we explore specific solutions throughout this book, maintaining this implementation mindset will help guide effective decision-making and successful deployment. Understanding both the possibilities and practical considerations of AI implementation creates the foundation for achieving meaningful results with AI solutions.

AI solutions span a broad spectrum of capabilities, each category addressing specific types of challenges. Understanding these categories provides crucial context for exploring specific solutions throughout our journey. This categorization helps organize our understanding while illuminating the relationships between different types of AI solutions.

Language AI solutions represent one of the most widely implemented categories. These solutions process and generate human language, enabling applications from document analysis to automated translation. The ability to work with natural language opens possibilities for improving communication, automating content creation, and enhancing information access. The evolution of language models has transformed how organizations interact with textual information.

AI TOOLBOX: EMPOWERING THE LEARNER

The foundation of language AI solutions lies in their ability to understand context and meaning in human communication. This understanding enables applications ranging from simple text classification to complex dialogue systems. The practical impact of these solutions continues to grow as their capabilities expand and implementation becomes more accessible.

Data AI solutions form another fundamental category, helping organizations extract value from their information resources. These solutions analyze patterns, identify trends, and generate insights from structured and unstructured data. Their capabilities extend from basic statistical analysis to complex predictive modeling. The ability to process and understand data at scale has transformed how organizations make decisions and operate.

The power of data AI solutions comes from their ability to identify patterns humans might miss. By processing vast amounts of information quickly and consistently, these solutions enable organizations to make more informed decisions. The practical applications range from business intelligence to scientific research, demonstrating the versatility of data-focused AI.

Audio and vision solutions process rich media content, interpreting sounds and images. Computer vision solutions analyze visual information, from simple image recognition to complex scene understanding. Audio processing solutions work with sound, enabling speech recognition, audio analysis, and sound generation. Together, these solutions help machines understand and interact with the world through sight and sound.

The evolution of audio and vision solutions has been particularly dramatic. Improvements in model architectures and training techniques have enabled increasingly sophisticated capabilities. These advances have made rich media processing more accessible while opening new possibilities for practical applications.

Healthcare AI solutions demonstrate how artificial intelligence addresses specialized domain needs. These solutions assist with tasks ranging from medical imaging analysis to patient data interpretation. Their implementation requires careful attention to accuracy, reliability, and regulatory compliance. The impact of these solutions continues to grow as healthcare organizations seek ways to improve patient care while managing increasing complexity.

The development of healthcare AI solutions shows how domain expertise combines with AI capabilities. These solutions must not only perform technical tasks effectively but also integrate seamlessly into healthcare workflows. This combination of technical capability and practical usability illustrates key principles of successful AI implementation.

Robotics AI solutions combine artificial intelligence with physical automation. These solutions enable robots to perceive their environment, make decisions, and interact with the physical world. Their applications range from industrial automation to specialized task assistance. The integration of AI with robotics creates new possibilities for automation and human-machine collaboration.

The practical impact of robotics AI solutions extends beyond traditional industrial applications. As these solutions become more sophisticated, they enable new forms of automation and assistance. Understanding their capabilities and limitations helps organizations evaluate potential applications effectively.

Gaming AI solutions create interactive experiences through intelligent behavior. These solutions control non-player characters, generate game content, and adapt gameplay experiences. Their implementation balances computational efficiency with engaging interaction. The gaming industry continues to drive innovation in AI, creating solutions that combine technical sophistication with practical application.

The development of gaming AI solutions demonstrates important principles of AI implementation. These solutions must operate in real-time, adapt to user actions, and create engaging experiences. Their evolution shows how technical capabilities can be shaped to meet specific practical requirements.

Cross-domain applications represent an emerging trend, combining multiple AI capabilities to address complex challenges. These solutions demonstrate how different AI technologies can work together, creating capabilities greater than the sum of their parts. Understanding how solutions can be combined helps organizations plan more comprehensive implementations.

Each solution category brings unique considerations for implementation. Some focus on processing efficiency, others on accuracy and reliability. Some require specialized hardware, while others operate primarily through software. Understanding these characteristics helps guide solution selection and implementation planning.

The relationships between categories create additional possibilities for innovation. Organizations often combine solutions from multiple categories to address complex challenges. Understanding these relationships helps guide the development of comprehensive AI strategies.

As we explore specific solutions in upcoming chapters, this categorical understanding will provide context for deeper investigation. Each category will reveal its unique capabilities, requirements, and best practices for implementation. This framework helps organize our exploration while highlighting the practical possibilities of AI solutions.

Building an effective AI strategy requires thoughtful planning and preparation. The successful implementation of AI solutions depends not just on selecting the right tools, but on creating a comprehensive framework for their effective use. This structured approach helps organizations move from possibility to practical reality.

Assessment begins with a clear understanding of current capabilities and needs. Organizations must evaluate their existing processes, technical infrastructure, and expertise. This baseline assessment helps identify both opportunities for AI implementation and potential challenges to address. Understanding the starting point proves crucial for planning effective implementation strategies.

Resource planning encompasses more than just budgetary considerations. Organizations must account for technical infrastructure requirements, from computational resources to data storage needs. Human resource planning proves equally important, identifying needed expertise and potential training requirements. Time represents another crucial resource, requiring realistic estimation for implementation phases.

The human element plays a central role in successful implementation. Organizations must consider both technical expertise requirements and change management needs. Training programs help build necessary skills, while clear communication helps manage expectations and build support for AI initiatives. Understanding and addressing human factors often determines implementation success.

Implementation planning benefits from a phased approach. Starting with pilot projects allows organizations to build experience while managing risks. Successful pilots provide valuable lessons for broader implementation while demonstrating value to stakeholders. This progressive approach helps build momentum while developing internal capabilities.

Success metrics must align with organizational objectives. Clear, measurable goals help guide implementation while providing concrete ways to evaluate progress. These metrics might include technical performance measures, business impact indicators, and user adoption rates. Regular evaluation against these metrics helps ensure implementations stay on track.

Risk management forms another crucial element of implementation planning. Organizations must identify potential challenges, from technical issues to adoption barriers. Mitigation strategies help address risks proactively, while contingency plans provide guidance when issues arise. This preparation helps create more resilient implementations.

The learning process continues throughout implementation. Organizations must stay informed about emerging capabilities and best practices. This ongoing education helps identify new opportunities while avoiding potential pitfalls. Building a culture of continuous learning supports long-term implementation success.

Integration with existing systems requires careful consideration. Organizations must understand how AI solutions will work with current tools and processes. Technical integration planning helps ensure smooth implementation, while process integration planning helps maximize solution effectiveness. This comprehensive approach helps create sustainable implementations.

Change management proves particularly important for AI implementation. New solutions often require adjustments to established workflows and practices. Clear communication, user training, and ongoing support help manage these transitions effectively. Understanding and addressing organizational change helps ensure successful adoption.

Cost considerations extend beyond initial implementation. Organizations must plan for ongoing operational expenses, maintenance requirements, and potential scaling costs. Understanding the total cost of ownership helps create sustainable implementation plans. This comprehensive view supports better decision-making throughout the implementation process.

Sustainability planning helps ensure long-term success. Organizations must consider how implementations will evolve over time, from scaling requirements to upgrade paths. This forward-looking approach helps create more adaptable solutions while managing long-term costs effectively.

Documentation plays a crucial role in implementation success. Clear records of decisions, processes, and lessons learned help build institutional knowledge. This documentation supports both current operations and future implementations while enabling effective knowledge transfer across the organization.

Security and compliance requirements demand careful attention. Organizations must understand relevant regulations and standards while implementing appropriate safeguards. This attention to security and compliance helps protect both the organization and its stakeholders.

Building internal expertise represents a crucial investment. Organizations must develop both technical knowledge and implementation experience. This capability development helps reduce dependence on external resources while improving long-term implementation success.

The strategic framework created through this planning process provides direction for practical implementation. It helps organizations move beyond theoretical possibilities to achieve tangible results with AI technology. This structured approach supports successful implementation while managing risks and resources effectively.

Looking toward tomorrow reveals both exciting possibilities and important considerations in AI development. The rapid pace of innovation continues to expand what's possible with AI solutions while making these capabilities increasingly accessible. This evolution shapes both immediate implementation opportunities and longer-term strategic planning.

Our journey through AI implementation builds upon the foundations established in Book One. Where we previously explored AI's nature and capabilities, we now move into the practical realm of solution implementation. This progression from understanding to application marks a crucial step in mastering AI technology.

The chapters ahead will explore specific AI solutions in detail, examining their practical applications and implementation considerations. We'll investigate language AI solutions that enable natural communication, data solutions that uncover valuable insights, and audio/vision solutions that process rich media content. Each exploration will focus on practical implementation while building comprehensive understanding.

Our investigation of healthcare applications will reveal how AI solutions assist medical professionals in improving patient care. The examination of robotics solutions will show how AI enables automation and human-machine collaboration. Our exploration of gaming applications will demonstrate how AI creates immersive interactive experiences. Throughout these investigations, practical implementation considerations will guide our learning.

Knowledge builds progressively through our journey. Each chapter adds new understanding while reinforcing core implementation principles. This layered approach helps develop both broad knowledge and specific expertise, creating a comprehensive foundation for successful AI implementation.

Technical understanding represents only part of our learning journey. Equally important is developing the judgment to select appropriate solutions and implement them effectively. This practical wisdom comes through understanding both successes and challenges in AI implementation.

Implementation success requires balancing multiple factors. Technical capabilities must align with organizational needs. Resource requirements must match available capacity. Integration plans must consider existing systems and processes. Our exploration will examine how successful implementations manage these considerations effectively.

The rapid evolution of AI technology ensures our journey will be dynamic. New solutions emerge regularly, expanding possibilities and creating fresh opportunities for innovation. Understanding core principles and evaluation methods helps navigate this evolving landscape while making informed decisions about AI implementation.

Practical implementation skills grow through progressive experience. Starting with foundational knowledge, we'll build understanding of specific solution types and their implementation requirements. This progression helps develop both technical expertise and practical judgment.

Success in this journey requires both knowledge and wisdom, knowing what's possible with AI solutions while understanding how to implement them responsibly and effectively. The chapters ahead will guide you through this process, providing the insights and understanding needed to leverage AI solutions successfully.

Our exploration maintains focus on practical value creation. Beyond understanding technical capabilities, we'll examine how AI solutions deliver tangible benefits. This emphasis on practical outcomes helps guide effective implementation decisions while ensuring solutions address real needs.

The journey ahead promises both challenges and opportunities. New capabilities will emerge, creating fresh possibilities for innovation. Implementation approaches will evolve, offering improved ways to leverage AI solutions. Maintaining both technical understanding and practical focus helps navigate these developments effectively.

Your role in this journey extends beyond passive learning. Active engagement with concepts and practical considerations helps develop deeper understanding. Questions and challenges encountered along the way contribute to learning while developing practical implementation skills.

The rapid pace of AI development creates ongoing learning opportunities. New solutions, improved implementation approaches, and emerging best practices continue to shape the AI landscape. This evolution makes continuous learning both necessary and rewarding.

Each step in our journey builds toward practical capability. From understanding solution categories to mastering implementation approaches, every chapter contributes to comprehensive AI literacy. This knowledge empowers informed decisions about AI implementation while guiding effective solution deployment.

Welcome to your journey through the AI toolbox. Together we'll explore the practical world of AI solutions, beginning with the fundamental building blocks: models that power AI capabilities, tools that enable their implementation, and platforms that bring them together. Let's begin our exploration of how these essential components combine to create powerful, practical AI solutions.

CHAPTER 2: MODELS, TOOLS, AND PLATFORMS EXPLAINED

In Book One of our AI journey, we explored the fundamental nature of artificial intelligence, understanding what AI is and how it has evolved. We examined its basic principles, ethical considerations, and potential impact on our world. That foundation of knowledge now serves as our launching point into the practical realm of AI implementation.

Where Book One answered the question "What is AI?" we now turn to the equally crucial question "How do we use AI?" This transition from understanding to implementation begins with a deeper look at the working components that make AI solutions possible: models that process information and generate outputs, tools that enable practical application, and platforms that bring everything together.

Think of these components as the building blocks of practical AI implementation. Models serve as the computational engines, processing information based on their training. Tools provide the means to work with these models effectively. Platforms create the environments where models and tools come together to solve real-world problems.

Understanding how these components work sets the stage for our exploration of specific AI solutions in upcoming chapters. When we examine language AI solutions, we'll build upon our knowledge of how models process information. Our investigation of data AI solutions will leverage our understanding of how tools analyze and visualize information. Each subsequent chapter will draw upon the practical foundation we establish here.

The journey ahead focuses squarely on implementation, taking us beyond theory into the realm of practical application. We'll examine not just what these components are, but how they work together to create functional AI solutions. This understanding proves crucial for the detailed implementation guidance provided throughout this book.

Let's begin our practical exploration with a closer look at these essential components, understanding how they work while preparing for the specific implementation strategies we'll explore in upcoming chapters.

In Book One, we explored the theoretical foundations of AI models, understanding their role in artificial intelligence. Now we examine how these models actually work, setting the stage for practical implementation. This transition from theory to practice reveals the operational aspects of AI models that drive real-world solutions.

AI models function as information processors, taking inputs and generating outputs based on learned patterns. Consider how a language model processes text: it receives words or phrases as input, analyzes them based on its training, and produces appropriate responses. This basic operational flow underlies all AI models, though specific implementations vary based on model type and purpose.

The evolution from early AI models to today's sophisticated systems parallels the progression from simple pattern matching to complex learning systems. Early models relied on predefined rules and limited pattern recognition.

Modern models employ advanced learning techniques, enabling them to discover and apply patterns from training data. This evolution has dramatically expanded the practical capabilities of AI models.

Machine learning models represent one fundamental category of AI models in practice. These models learn from examples, discovering patterns that enable them to make predictions or decisions about new information. Their operation involves processing input data through learned patterns to generate useful outputs. This ability to learn from examples rather than following explicit programming makes machine learning models particularly versatile.

Neural networks build upon these capabilities, organizing processing units in layers that enable more sophisticated pattern recognition. Each layer processes information in specific ways, transforming inputs through multiple stages to produce final outputs. This layered processing enables neural networks to handle complex tasks like image recognition or natural language understanding.

Deep learning models extend this architecture with additional layers and sophisticated processing techniques. These models can discover intricate patterns in data, enabling them to handle tasks that require nuanced understanding or complex decision-making. Their practical operation involves processing information through numerous specialized layers, each contributing to the final output.

Understanding how models process information proves crucial for practical implementation. Models receive input data, process it through their learned patterns, and generate corresponding outputs. This processing can involve various operations: classification tasks sort inputs into categories, regression tasks predict numerical values, and generation tasks create new content based on learned patterns.

The relationship between models and data shapes their practical operation. Models learn patterns from training data, which influences their capabilities and limitations. The quality and relevance of training data significantly affects model performance. This relationship between models and data underlies many practical considerations in AI implementation.

Model architecture determines how information flows through the system. Some architectures excel at processing sequential data like text or time series. Others handle spatial relationships in images or complex patterns in structured data. Understanding these architectural characteristics helps guide model selection for specific applications.

Operational requirements vary across model types. Some models need substantial computational resources for training but operate efficiently once trained. Others require less intensive training but more resources during operation. These practical considerations influence both model selection and implementation planning.

Performance characteristics play a crucial role in practical application. Models exhibit different levels of accuracy, speed, and resource efficiency. Some models prioritize processing speed over absolute accuracy, while others emphasize precision at the cost of computational efficiency. Understanding these tradeoffs helps match models to specific needs.

The capabilities of AI models extend beyond simple input-output processing. Many models can learn continuously, improving their performance with exposure to new data. Some can transfer learning from one domain to another, while others excel at identifying unusual patterns or anomalies. These capabilities create diverse possibilities for practical application.

Limitations also shape practical implementation. Models operate effectively only within their trained domains. They require careful validation to ensure reliable performance. Understanding these limitations helps set realistic expectations and plan appropriate implementation strategies.

As we explore specific AI solutions in upcoming chapters, this understanding of model operation will prove invaluable.

AI TOOLBOX: EMPOWERING THE LEARNER

When we examine language AI solutions, we'll build upon our knowledge of how models process textual information. Our exploration of vision AI will leverage our understanding of how models handle visual data. Each implementation will draw upon this foundational knowledge of model operation.

This practical understanding of AI models sets the stage for examining the tools that enable their implementation. While models provide the computational capabilities, tools make these capabilities accessible and usable. Let's explore how these essential components work together in creating effective AI solutions.

Moving from models to their practical application, AI tools provide the bridge between computational capability and usable solutions. While models perform the core processing, tools make these capabilities accessible and practical for real-world use. Understanding how tools work prepares us for implementing specific solutions in upcoming chapters.

AI tools serve multiple functions in practical implementation. Development tools help create and modify models. Deployment tools enable model implementation in production environments. Management tools monitor and maintain operational solutions. Each tool type plays a specific role in bringing AI capabilities to life.

The tool ecosystem has evolved significantly with AI technology. Early tools required extensive technical expertise and provided limited functionality. Modern tools offer more accessible interfaces and automated capabilities, making AI implementation practical for a broader range of users. This evolution continues to reduce implementation barriers while expanding practical possibilities.

Development tools form a crucial category in practical implementation. These tools help prepare data, train models, and validate results. They provide interfaces for working with model architectures and managing training processes. Understanding how development tools work helps guide effective model creation and modification.

Implementation tools enable practical deployment of AI capabilities. These tools handle tasks like model integration, performance optimization, and scaling. They provide mechanisms for incorporating AI capabilities into existing systems and workflows. This integration role makes implementation tools essential for practical AI solutions.

Management tools support operational AI solutions. They monitor performance, track resource usage, and manage updates. These tools help maintain solution reliability while enabling continuous improvement. Understanding management tool capabilities helps plan effective operational strategies.

The working relationship between tools and models shapes practical implementation. Tools must match model requirements and operational characteristics. They need to handle appropriate data formats and processing flows. This alignment between tools and models significantly influences implementation success.

Tool selection considerations extend beyond basic functionality. Integration capabilities affect how tools work with existing systems. Resource requirements influence operational costs and scaling potential. User interface characteristics impact tool accessibility and adoption. Understanding these practical aspects helps guide effective tool selection.

The operational nature of AI tools continues to evolve. New capabilities emerge as technology advances. Automation reduces manual intervention requirements. Integration options expand implementation possibilities. This evolution creates new opportunities while requiring ongoing attention to tool capabilities and requirements.

Consider how tools function in practical implementation. Data preparation tools help organize and clean information for model training. Development environments provide spaces for creating and testing solutions. Deployment tools manage the transition from development to production. Each tool type contributes specific capabilities to the implementation process.

Tool architecture influences practical operation. Some tools operate as standalone applications, while others form part of larger development environments. Some focus on specific tasks, while others provide comprehensive functionality. Understanding these architectural differences helps guide tool selection and implementation planning.

The interaction between tools shapes implementation workflows. Data moves between preparation tools, development environments, and deployment systems. Management tools monitor operations across multiple components. Understanding these interactions helps create effective implementation processes.

As we explore specific solutions in upcoming chapters, this understanding of tool operation will prove essential. Language AI implementations will use specific tools for text processing and model interaction. Vision AI solutions will employ tools designed for image processing and analysis. Each implementation will leverage appropriate tools for its specific requirements.

The practical impact of tools extends beyond technical implementation. Tools influence development efficiency, operational reliability, and user adoption. They affect implementation costs and scaling capabilities. Understanding these practical implications helps guide tool selection and implementation planning.

Looking ahead to our exploration of specific solutions, this foundation in tool operation provides crucial context. We'll see how different tools enable particular implementations while understanding why specific tools suit certain applications. This knowledge helps guide effective solution development and deployment.

Having explored models and tools, we now examine the environments where they come together: AI platforms. These platforms provide the infrastructure and systems necessary for practical AI implementation. Understanding how platforms work establishes crucial context for the specific implementations we'll explore in upcoming chapters.

AI platforms serve as comprehensive environments for AI development and deployment. They provide the computational resources, storage systems, and management capabilities needed to work with AI solutions effectively. This infrastructure role makes platforms fundamental to practical AI implementation.

The core architecture of AI platforms involves multiple integrated systems. Computing resources handle processing requirements for model training and operation. Storage systems manage data and model assets. Management systems coordinate resource allocation and monitor performance. These systems work together to support AI solution development and deployment.

Development environments within platforms provide spaces for creating and testing AI solutions. They offer access to necessary tools and resources while managing technical complexity. These environments help streamline development processes while ensuring access to required capabilities.

Resource management represents a crucial platform function. Platforms allocate computing power, memory, and storage based on operational needs. They manage these resources efficiently, scaling them to match changing requirements. This dynamic resource management helps optimize both performance and cost.

Integration systems enable platforms to work with various tools and technologies. They provide mechanisms for connecting different components and managing data flow between systems. These integration capabilities help create cohesive solutions from diverse components.

Platform operation involves continuous monitoring and management. Performance tracking systems observe resource usage and system behavior. Management tools handle updates and maintenance tasks. These operational capabilities help maintain reliable solution performance.

Security systems protect platform operations and assets. They manage access control, protect sensitive data, and maintain operational integrity. Understanding these security aspects helps plan appropriate implementation strategies.

Consider how platforms support practical implementation. They provide environments for developing solutions, resources for operating them, and systems for managing them. This comprehensive support makes platforms essential for substantial AI implementations.

The relationship between platforms and other components shapes implementation possibilities. Platforms must support appropriate tools and model types. They need to provide necessary resources and capabilities. This alignment between platforms and components significantly influences implementation success.

Platform capabilities continue to evolve with technology advancement. New features emerge, performance improves, and integration options expand. Understanding this evolution helps organizations plan effective platform strategies.

Operational considerations extend beyond basic functionality. Scaling capabilities affect growth potential. Integration options influence implementation possibilities. Resource management affects operational costs. Understanding these practical aspects helps guide platform selection and usage.

As we explore specific solutions in upcoming chapters, this understanding of platform operation will prove valuable. Different implementations will leverage various platform capabilities, from computational resources to management tools. Each solution type will demonstrate how platforms support practical AI implementation.

The foundation we've built in understanding platform operations illuminates the path ahead. As we delve deeper into specific solutions throughout this book, we'll see how different types of AI applications leverage platform capabilities in unique ways. This knowledge of platform functionality serves as a crucial steppingstone toward successful AI implementation, preparing us for the practical journey ahead.

Within the AI ecosystem, development platforms serve as essential hubs for creating, sharing, and implementing AI solutions. These platforms provide structured environments where developers can access resources, collaborate on projects, and deploy AI applications. Understanding how these platforms work proves crucial for practical AI implementation.

GitHub stands as a fundamental platform in AI development. As a version control and collaboration platform, GitHub provides crucial infrastructure for AI development through several key mechanisms. At its core, GitHub enables developers to maintain organized collections of code, models, and documentation within repositories. Each repository contains complete AI projects, including source code, configuration files, and implementation instructions. This organization helps maintain project clarity while enabling effective collaboration.

The platform's version control system, built on Git, tracks changes to AI projects over time with remarkable precision. Developers can maintain different versions of models or applications, experiment with new features, and roll back changes when needed. This versioning capability proves especially valuable when developing and refining AI solutions, as it maintains a complete history of project evolution.

GitHub's collaboration framework centers around its pull request system, which enables structured participation in AI projects. Developers can propose changes, review others' contributions, and merge improvements into main project branches. This systematic approach to collaboration helps maintain code quality while enabling community participation in development efforts.

Project organization within GitHub relies on sophisticated

tracking and management tools. Teams can monitor issues, coordinate development activities, and maintain clear project timelines. The platform's integrated wiki system and documentation features ensure that knowledge about implementations remains accessible and up to date.

Automation capabilities through GitHub Actions enable sophisticated workflow management for AI projects. Teams can automate testing procedures, streamline deployment processes, and maintain consistent quality checks throughout development. This automation reduces manual overhead while ensuring reliable project maintenance.

Hugging Face represents another crucial development platform, with specific focus on machine learning and AI models. The platform maintains an extensive repository of pre-trained AI models, particularly concentrating on natural language processing and machine learning applications. This comprehensive collection enables developers to access and utilize existing models rather than building from scratch.

The model management system within Hugging Face provides sophisticated tools for uploading, versioning, and sharing AI models. Developers can maintain different versions of their models while tracking changes and improvements over time. This versioning capability proves essential for maintaining model quality and enabling collaborative development.

Dataset management forms another cornerstone of Hugging Face's offerings. The platform maintains a comprehensive collection of datasets suitable for AI model training and testing. These resources span various domains and applications, providing crucial materials for AI development and validation.

Implementation support within Hugging Face includes robust libraries and tools for working with AI models effectively. These resources help developers with model loading, fine-tuning, and deployment tasks. The platform's documentation system provides detailed guidance for model implementation, including practical examples and technical specifications.

The community aspects of both platforms play crucial roles in AI development. Developers can engage in technical discussions, share implementation insights, and collaborate on improvements. This knowledge sharing accelerates development while improving solution quality through collective expertise.

Both platforms implement sophisticated access control mechanisms to protect resources and manage collaboration effectively. Security features safeguard code, models, and other assets while enabling appropriate sharing and cooperation. Integration capabilities allow these platforms to work seamlessly with other development tools and environments.

The practical impact of these development platforms extends throughout the AI implementation process. They enable efficient knowledge sharing, promote resource reuse, and help maintain high solution quality. Their structured environments support systematic development while enabling innovation through collaboration.

Understanding individual components provides essential knowledge, but successful AI implementation requires understanding how these components work together. The integration of models, tools, and platforms creates functional AI solutions. This understanding of component relationships sets the foundation for the specific implementations we'll explore in upcoming chapters.

Models and tools interact through defined interfaces and data flows. Tools provide the means to work with models effectively, handling tasks like data preparation, model training, and result analysis. This interaction enables practical application of model capabilities while managing technical complexity.

Tools and platforms maintain ongoing connections that support development and deployment. Platforms provide the resources tools need to function effectively, while tools enable practical use of platform capabilities. This reciprocal relationship creates functional development and operational environments.

Platforms and repositories establish links that enable resource sharing and management. These connections facilitate access to models, tools, and development resources while maintaining appropriate controls. Understanding these relationships helps create effective implementation strategies.

The flow of data between components follows established patterns. Input data moves through preparation tools to models for processing. Results flow through analysis tools for interpretation and presentation. Understanding these patterns helps guide effective solution design.

Component communication uses standard methods and protocols. These mechanisms enable reliable interaction while maintaining security and performance. Understanding these communication methods helps ensure reliable solution operation.

Consider how components work together in practical implementation. Data preparation tools feed information to models for processing. Development tools interact with platforms to access necessary resources. Management tools monitor operations across components. Each interaction contributes to overall solution functionality.

Integration requirements influence component selection and configuration. Components must support necessary interfaces and protocols. They need compatible data formats and processing methods. Understanding these requirements helps guide effective component selection.

The relationships between components shape implementation possibilities. Available interfaces affect integration options. Resource requirements influence operational capabilities. Understanding these relationships helps guide implementation planning.

Component integration continues to evolve with

technology advancement. New integration methods emerge, capabilities expand, and automation increases. This evolution creates new implementation possibilities while requiring attention to integration capabilities.

Implementation considerations extend beyond technical integration. Security requirements affect component interaction. Performance needs influence integration methods. Understanding these practical aspects helps guide integration planning.

As we explore specific solutions in upcoming chapters, this understanding of component integration will prove essential. Different implementations will demonstrate various integration approaches, from simple data flows to complex multi-component systems. Each solution type will show how integrated components create practical AI capabilities.

Looking ahead to our examination of specific AI solutions, this foundation in component integration provides crucial context. We'll see how different solutions leverage component integration while understanding why particular approaches suit specific applications. This knowledge helps guide effective solution development and deployment.

The practical impact of component integration extends throughout implementation. Integration choices affect development efficiency, operational reliability, and system maintainability. Understanding these implications helps create effective implementation strategies.

Our exploration of models, tools, and platforms has established the foundational understanding needed for practical AI implementation. We've seen how models provide the computational capabilities that drive AI solutions, how tools make these capabilities accessible and manageable, and how platforms create the environments where development and deployment occur. We've examined the ecosystems where these components come together and understood how their integration creates functional solutions.

This knowledge forms the bridge between the theoretical

understanding developed in Book One and the practical implementations we'll explore throughout this book. As we move forward to examine different types of AI solutions, from language processing to computer vision, from healthcare applications to gaming systems, this understanding of core components will illuminate how each solution type leverages specific capabilities for practical results.

Our next chapter explores another crucial aspect of AI implementation: the choice between open source and proprietary solutions. This decision significantly influences how organizations approach AI implementation, affecting everything from development flexibility to operational costs. Armed with our understanding of models, tools, and platforms, we're prepared to examine these options and their implications for practical AI implementation.

GIL OREN

CHAPTER 3: OPEN SOURCE VS PROPRIETARY AI

Having explored the fundamental components of AI implementation, we now turn to a crucial decision that shapes how organizations approach AI development: the choice between open source and proprietary solutions. This decision influences not just tool selection, but entire implementation strategies and development approaches.

Our examination of development platforms like GitHub and Hugging Face in the previous chapter revealed how both open source and proprietary models can coexist within the AI ecosystem. While GitHub enables open collaboration on AI projects, many of the solutions hosted there implement different licensing approaches. Similarly, Hugging Face hosts both open source models freely available for modification and proprietary models with specific usage restrictions.

This interplay between open source and proprietary approaches appears throughout the AI landscape. Language models demonstrate this range clearly, from open source alternatives that enable full customization to proprietary solutions like ChatGPT that provide powerful capabilities through controlled interfaces. Similar patterns emerge across all categories of AI solutions we'll explore in upcoming chapters.

Understanding the implications of choosing between open source and proprietary solutions provides essential context for our later exploration of specific AI applications. Whether implementing language processing, computer vision, or specialized domain solutions, organizations must navigate these licensing considerations while building their AI capabilities.

Let us examine how these different approaches to AI development and distribution shape implementation possibilities, influence resource requirements, and affect long-term solution sustainability. This understanding will prove crucial as we explore specific solution categories in the chapters ahead.

The foundation of any AI implementation begins with understanding the licensing models that govern how solutions can be used, modified, and distributed. These models shape not just immediate implementation options but long-term development possibilities and organizational responsibilities.

Open source licensing in AI reflects principles established throughout software development history. These licenses grant users specific freedoms: the ability to study how solutions work, modify them for specific needs, and share improvements with others. The GNU General Public License (GPL), MIT License, and Apache License represent common frameworks that formalize these rights while establishing clear usage requirements.

Proprietary licensing takes a different approach, protecting intellectual property while enabling controlled solution distribution. These licenses typically restrict modification rights, limit distribution capabilities, and maintain vendor control over solution development. Companies may offer different licensing tiers, from individual usage to enterprise deployment, each with specific terms and conditions.

AI TOOLBOX: EMPOWERING THE LEARNER

The evolution of AI licensing models parallels the technology's development. Early AI solutions often emerged from academic and research environments, favoring open source approaches that enabled knowledge sharing and collaborative improvement. As commercial applications grew, proprietary models emerged to protect investments and support sustainable development.

Consider how these models manifest in practice. TensorFlow, an open source machine learning framework, enables developers to examine its internal workings, modify its functionality, and contribute improvements back to the community. In contrast, proprietary solutions like certain cloud-based AI services provide powerful capabilities through controlled interfaces while maintaining code privacy.

The implications of licensing choices extend throughout solution lifecycles. Open source licenses typically require derivative works to maintain similar freedoms, ensuring continued community access to improvements. Proprietary licenses might restrict modification rights but often include support and maintenance guarantees not typically available with open source solutions.

Legal considerations play crucial roles in licensing decisions. Open source licenses contain specific obligations regarding code sharing and attribution. Proprietary licenses include terms about usage rights, liability limitations, and confidentiality requirements. Understanding these legal aspects helps organizations maintain compliance while leveraging AI capabilities effectively.

The relationship between licensing models and development approaches significantly influences implementation strategies. Open source solutions often enable deep customization but require internal expertise for modification and maintenance. Proprietary solutions might limit customization options but provide professional support and established upgrade paths.

Cost structures vary significantly between licensing

models. Open source solutions typically involve no direct licensing costs but may require substantial investment in development and maintenance resources. Proprietary solutions often include licensing fees but might reduce overall development costs through included support and maintenance services.

Security considerations differ between approaches. Open source solutions enable thorough security auditing through code visibility but require organizational dedication to security maintenance. Proprietary solutions might offer professional security management but require trust in vendor practices and responsiveness.

The impact of licensing decisions extends beyond immediate implementation. They affect long-term maintenance options, upgrade possibilities, and vendor relationships. Understanding these implications helps organizations make informed decisions aligned with their strategic objectives.

Licensing models continue to evolve with AI technology. New hybrid approaches emerge, combining aspects of both open source and proprietary models. Understanding this evolution helps organizations adapt their strategies while maintaining effective AI implementations.

The choice between licensing models often reflects broader organizational strategies. Some organizations prioritize control and customization possibilities through open source solutions. Others value the support and reliability guarantees of proprietary options. Many implement both approaches based on specific solution requirements.

The development community plays different roles under various licensing models. Open source communities contribute improvements, share knowledge, and collaborate on solution development. Proprietary solution communities might focus more on implementation strategies and usage optimization within license constraints.

As we explore specific solutions in upcoming chapters, this

understanding of licensing models will provide crucial context. Whether examining language processing solutions, computer vision systems, or specialized applications, licensing considerations influence implementation options and strategies.

Open source AI solutions represent a fundamental approach to artificial intelligence development and implementation. By providing access to source code, enabling modification rights, and fostering community collaboration, these solutions create unique opportunities for innovation and customization.

The core principles of open source AI extend beyond simple code access. The Open Source Initiative defines essential freedoms: the right to use software for any purpose, to study how it works, to modify it for specific needs, and to distribute modifications to help others. Major open source AI projects like TensorFlow and PyTorch embody these principles, enabling broad community participation in their development and evolution.

Community development drives open source AI advancement. Contributors worldwide participate in improving solutions, fixing issues, and expanding capabilities. This collaborative approach often leads to rapid innovation and robust solutions. Projects hosted on GitHub demonstrate this dynamic, with developers proposing improvements through pull requests, discussing implementations in issue threads, and sharing knowledge through documentation.

Source code availability enables deep understanding and customization. Organizations can examine exactly how solutions work, modify them for specific requirements, and ensure they meet particular needs. This transparency proves especially valuable in AI implementation, where understanding model behavior and adapting solutions to specific use cases often proves crucial for success.

Documentation in open source projects typically evolves through community effort. Contributors share implementation experiences, document features, and provide usage examples. While documentation quality can vary, popular projects often maintain comprehensive guides and examples. TensorFlow's extensive documentation, for instance, combines official guidance with community contributions.

Support for open source AI solutions comes through multiple channels. Community forums enable users to seek help, share experiences, and solve problems collaboratively. Many projects maintain official communication channels for user support and development coordination. Some organizations also offer professional support services for popular open source solutions.

The development process in open source AI projects follows established patterns. Changes typically undergo peer review through pull requests, ensuring quality and consistency. Testing frameworks validate modifications, while continuous integration systems ensure solution stability. This structured approach helps maintain solution reliability despite distributed development.

Security management in open source solutions involves community vigilance. Code visibility enables thorough security auditing, while community members can identify and address vulnerabilities. Many projects maintain security teams and formal processes for handling security issues. This collaborative security approach often leads to rapid vulnerability resolution.

Training resources for open source AI solutions often emerge from community efforts. Users share learning materials, create tutorials, and document implementation approaches. These resources, combined with access to source code, enable organizations to build internal expertise effectively.

Implementation flexibility represents a key advantage of open source AI solutions. Organizations can modify solutions for specific needs, integrate them with existing systems, and adapt them as requirements evolve. This flexibility proves particularly valuable when standard solutions don't precisely match organizational needs.

Cost considerations with open source AI extend beyond the absence of licensing fees. Organizations must consider resources needed for implementation, maintenance, and support. While avoiding license costs, successful open source implementation often requires investment in technical expertise and development resources.

Distribution rights under open source licenses enable solution sharing. Organizations can distribute modified versions, though specific requirements vary by license type. This ability to share improvements benefits the broader community while enabling collaborative solution development.

Version control practices in open source AI development enable systematic evolution. Projects typically maintain multiple branches for development, testing, and stable releases. This structured approach helps organizations manage solution updates while maintaining stable implementations.

Quality assurance in open source projects combines automated testing with community review. Continuous integration systems verify code functionality, while peer review processes ensure implementation quality. This multi-layered approach helps maintain solution reliability despite distributed development.

Governance models in major open source AI projects provide development direction. Projects might operate under organizational foundations, corporate sponsorship, or community governance. Understanding these models helps organizations evaluate long-term solution sustainability.

As we examine specific AI applications in upcoming chapters, many will incorporate open source components. Understanding how these solutions operate, their development processes, and their implementation requirements will prove crucial for successful deployment.

Proprietary AI solutions represent a distinct approach to artificial intelligence development and distribution, one built on controlled access, professional support, and sustained development investment. These solutions provide organizations with tested, supported implementations while maintaining vendor control over core technologies.

The fundamental structure of proprietary AI reflects careful balance between capability provision and intellectual property protection. Companies invest substantial resources in research, development, and optimization, protecting these investments through licensing restrictions and access controls. This model enables sustained development while ensuring solution quality through controlled evolution.

Consider how major proprietary solutions demonstrate this approach. ChatGPT, for instance, provides powerful language capabilities through carefully managed interfaces. While users can access sophisticated AI functionality, the underlying models and training methods remain protected. This controlled access enables consistent service delivery while maintaining technological advantages.

Professional development processes characterize proprietary AI solutions. Companies maintain dedicated development teams, implement systematic testing procedures, and follow structured release cycles. This organized approach helps ensure solution reliability while enabling consistent feature enhancement. Internal quality control processes verify functionality before releases reach customers.

Documentation for proprietary solutions typically maintains professional standards throughout development. Technical writers create comprehensive guides, usage examples, and implementation documentation. Regular updates ensure documentation matches current functionality. This systematic approach to documentation helps organizations implement solutions effectively while reducing support requirements.

Support systems for proprietary AI solutions often operate

on multiple levels. Technical support teams handle implementation issues and operational problems. Professional services groups assist with complex implementations. Account management teams help organizations maximize solution value. This layered support approach helps ensure implementation success.

Version control in proprietary solutions follows careful management practices. Development teams maintain internal repositories, manage feature branches, and coordinate releases. Beta testing programs enable controlled feature validation. This structured approach helps maintain solution stability while enabling consistent evolution.

Security management in proprietary AI solutions involves dedicated security teams and systematic processes. Regular security audits identify potential vulnerabilities. Dedicated incident response teams handle security issues. This professional security management helps protect both vendor systems and customer implementations.

Training resources for proprietary solutions often combine official materials with certified programs. Vendors provide implementation guides, best practices documentation, and usage examples. Certification programs validate expertise levels. This structured approach to knowledge sharing helps organizations build necessary implementation capabilities.

Implementation flexibility in proprietary solutions varies by vendor and license type. Some solutions enable significant customization within defined parameters. Others maintain stricter control over solution modification. Understanding these boundaries helps organizations plan effective implementations while maintaining vendor support.

Cost structures for proprietary AI solutions extend beyond basic licensing fees. Implementation costs might include professional services, support contracts, and usage-based charges. Enterprise agreements might provide broader access with different pricing models. Understanding total cost implications helps organizations plan effective

implementations.

Distribution restrictions form core elements of proprietary licensing. Solutions typically limit redistribution rights while controlling modification capabilities. Some licenses might enable limited sharing within organizational boundaries. Understanding these restrictions helps organizations maintain compliance while leveraging solution capabilities.

Integration capabilities in proprietary solutions often follow standardized approaches. Vendors provide documented APIs, integration frameworks, and connection tools. Professional services teams might assist with complex integrations. This structured approach helps organizations incorporate solutions into existing systems effectively.

Upgrade processes in proprietary solutions typically follow vendor-defined paths. Regular updates provide new features and security improvements. Version upgrades might require careful planning and vendor assistance. Understanding these processes helps organizations maintain current capabilities while managing upgrade complexity.

Vendor relationships play crucial roles in proprietary solution success. Account teams help organizations understand roadmap plans and capability evolution. Customer feedback programs enable feature requests and improvement suggestions. These relationships help align solution evolution with customer needs.

Performance optimization in proprietary solutions combines vendor expertise with customer requirements. Professional services teams might assist with configuration optimization. Monitoring tools track solution performance. This collaborative approach helps organizations achieve optimal solution operation.

Resource requirements for proprietary solutions often focus on implementation rather than development expertise. Organizations might need specialists familiar with vendor platforms rather than core development teams. Support contracts often provide access to vendor expertise when needed. This arrangement helps organizations focus on using rather than maintaining solutions.

The evolution of proprietary AI solutions often reflects market demands and technological advancement. Vendors invest in research and development to maintain competitive advantages. Regular releases incorporate new capabilities and improvements. This ongoing evolution helps organizations access current AI capabilities without internal development investment.

Compliance management in proprietary solutions often includes built-in capabilities. Solutions might incorporate regulatory compliance features. Vendor teams help organizations understand compliance implications. This support for compliance requirements helps organizations maintain regulatory alignment while leveraging AI capabilities.

Long-term strategy considerations with proprietary solutions include vendor stability assessment, roadmap alignment, and relationship management. Organizations must evaluate vendor longevity and commitment to solution evolution. Understanding these strategic aspects helps guide successful implementation planning.

The comparison between open source and proprietary AI solutions reveals nuanced differences that significantly impact implementation success. Understanding these differences helps organizations make informed decisions aligned with their specific needs, capabilities, and objectives. This comparison extends beyond simple feature lists to encompass total impact on organizational AI implementation.

Development speed varies significantly between solution types based on several factors. Open source solutions often benefit from rapid community innovation, with worldwide contributors proposing and implementing improvements. Proprietary solutions maintain systematic development cycles with regular feature releases. The TensorFlow ecosystem demonstrates rapid open source evolution, while platforms like ChatGPT show controlled but consistent proprietary development.

Quality assurance approaches differ fundamentally between solution types. Open source projects rely on community testing, peer review, and public issue tracking to maintain quality. Proprietary solutions implement systematic testing protocols with dedicated quality assurance teams. Both approaches can produce reliable solutions, though through distinctly different mechanisms.

Initial implementation speed often favors proprietary solutions with their structured onboarding processes and professional support systems. Open source solutions might require more initial setup time but offer greater customization potential. Organizations must weigh immediate deployment needs against long-term flexibility requirements when evaluating implementation approaches.

Security management demonstrates different strengths in each approach. Open source solutions enable thorough code review and rapid community response to vulnerabilities. Proprietary solutions provide professional security teams and systematic vulnerability management. Understanding these security approaches helps organizations align solution choice with their security requirements.

Cost structures reveal complex differences between solution types. Open source solutions eliminate licensing fees but often require significant internal expertise and development resources. Proprietary solutions include licensing costs but might reduce overall resource requirements through professional support and maintained functionality. Total cost analysis must consider both direct and indirect expenses.

Support systems operate differently between solution types. Open source solutions rely on community forums, documentation, and optional commercial support services. Proprietary solutions provide dedicated support teams, account management, and professional services. Organizations must evaluate their support needs and internal capabilities when comparing options.

Integration capabilities follow different patterns in each approach. Open source solutions enable deep integration through code access and modification rights. Proprietary solutions provide documented APIs and integration frameworks with vendor support. Integration requirements significantly influence solution selection and implementation planning.

Customization possibilities vary substantially between approaches. Open source solutions allow unlimited modification but require internal expertise to implement changes. Proprietary solutions might limit customization options while providing professional assistance for allowed modifications. Organizations must align customization needs with available resources.

Documentation quality and maintenance follow different models. Open source projects combine community contributions with project maintenance efforts. Proprietary solutions maintain professional documentation teams and systematic updates. Both approaches can produce comprehensive documentation, though maintenance methods differ significantly.

Risk management considerations differ between solution types. Open source solutions might present continuity risks if community support diminishes. Proprietary solutions carry vendor dependency risks and potential cost increase concerns. Understanding and planning for these risks helps organizations make informed decisions.

Performance optimization possibilities vary between approaches. Open source solutions enable deep optimization through code access but require significant expertise. Proprietary solutions might offer professional optimization services while limiting direct modification options. Performance requirements influence solution selection and implementation planning.

Compliance management capabilities differ significantly.

Open source solutions enable thorough compliance verification through code review but require internal expertise. Proprietary solutions often include compliance features with vendor guidance. Regulatory requirements often influence solution selection decisions.

Scalability options follow different patterns in each approach. Open source solutions enable unlimited scaling but require infrastructure management expertise. Proprietary solutions might include managed scaling options with usage-based pricing. Scaling requirements and operational capabilities influence solution selection.

Knowledge retention varies between solution types. Open source solutions enable deep understanding through code access but require systematic knowledge management. Proprietary solutions might limit deep system knowledge while providing comprehensive operational documentation. Organizations must consider knowledge management requirements when evaluating options.

Community engagement opportunities differ substantially. Open source solutions enable direct community participation and knowledge sharing. Proprietary solutions often provide user communities focused on implementation practices. Community engagement preferences influence solution selection and implementation planning.

Long-term sustainability follows different patterns. Open source solutions depend on community vitality and ongoing contribution. Proprietary solutions rely on vendor business success and market position. Organizations must evaluate long-term solution sustainability when making selection decisions.

Innovation potential varies between approaches. Open source solutions enable unlimited innovation through code access and modification rights. Proprietary solutions innovate through vendor research and development investments. Innovation requirements influence solution selection and implementation planning.

Technical debt management differs significantly. Open source solutions allow direct technical debt management but require internal expertise. Proprietary solutions often handle technical debt through vendor upgrade cycles. Understanding technical debt implications helps guide solution selection.

The future evolution of both solution types continues to shape implementation possibilities. Open source communities advance capabilities through collaborative development. Proprietary vendors invest in research and capability enhancement. Organizations must consider evolution patterns when planning long-term AI strategies.

Implementation considerations for AI solutions extend far beyond initial selection decisions, encompassing the entire lifecycle of solution deployment and operation. Organizations must carefully evaluate resource requirements, technical needs, and operational implications for both open source and proprietary implementations to ensure long-term success.

Resource planning reveals significant differences between implementation approaches. Open source implementations often require substantial internal technical expertise, including development teams familiar with AI technologies and specific frameworks. Proprietary implementations might focus more on solution administrators and integration specialists. Consider how major organizations often maintain dedicated teams for TensorFlow implementations, while proprietary solution deployments might primarily involve configuration specialists.

Infrastructure requirements vary considerably between solution types. Open source implementations might require extensive computational resources under direct organizational control. Proprietary cloud-based solutions often provide managed infrastructure but require reliable network connectivity. Organizations must evaluate their infrastructure capabilities and requirements when planning implementations.

Technical expertise needs differ fundamentally between approaches. Open source implementations often require deep technical knowledge of AI frameworks, development practices, and system optimization. Proprietary implementations might focus more on platform-specific knowledge and integration expertise. Understanding these expertise requirements helps organizations prepare appropriate technical teams.

Training requirements extend throughout implementation lifecycles. Open source implementations often need ongoing technical training as solutions evolve and new capabilities emerge. Proprietary implementations might focus more on platform-specific training and certification programs. Organizations must plan for continuous learning and skill development regardless of chosen approach.

Integration challenges manifest differently across solution types. Open source implementations enable deep integration through code access but require substantial technical effort. Proprietary solutions provide structured integration paths but might limit integration options. Organizations must evaluate their integration requirements and capabilities when planning implementations.

Operational support structures vary significantly between approaches. Open source implementations often require internal support capabilities with deep technical knowledge. Proprietary implementations might rely more on vendor support with internal platform expertise. Organizations must develop appropriate support structures aligned with their chosen implementation approach.

Monitoring requirements persist across solution types but follow different patterns. Open source implementations might require custom monitoring solutions and internal expertise. Proprietary solutions often provide integrated monitoring tools with vendor support. Organizations must establish effective monitoring regardless of implementation approach.

Security implementation varies between solution types. Open source implementations require comprehensive security management from internal teams. Proprietary solutions might include security features but still require internal security oversight. Organizations must establish appropriate security measures regardless of chosen approach.

Compliance requirements influence implementation approaches significantly. Open source implementations enable thorough compliance verification but require substantial documentation effort. Proprietary solutions might include compliance features but require careful verification. Organizations must maintain appropriate compliance regardless of implementation choice.

Documentation practices differ between solution types but remain crucial for success. Open source implementations often require extensive internal documentation of customizations and operational procedures. Proprietary implementations might focus more on platform-specific procedures and integration documentation. Organizations must maintain comprehensive documentation regardless of approach.

Change management processes vary between implementation types. Open source solutions enable unlimited changes but require careful management of modifications. Proprietary solutions might limit changes but provide structured update processes. Organizations must establish appropriate change management procedures aligned with their implementation approach.

Performance optimization requires different approaches across solution types. Open source implementations enable deep optimization but require significant expertise. Proprietary solutions might offer professional optimization services with limited customization options. Organizations must establish appropriate performance management processes regardless of approach.

Disaster recovery planning varies between implementation types. Open source implementations might require comprehensive internal recovery capabilities. Proprietary solutions often include disaster recovery features but require careful testing and verification. Organizations must establish appropriate recovery capabilities regardless of chosen approach.

Cost management practices differ significantly between solution types. Open source implementations often focus on resource and expertise costs. Proprietary implementations might emphasize license and usage costs. Organizations must establish appropriate cost management procedures aligned with their implementation approach.

Scalability management varies between solution types but remains crucial for success. Open source implementations enable unlimited scaling but require significant expertise. Proprietary solutions might provide managed scaling with usage-based pricing. Organizations must establish appropriate scaling procedures regardless of implementation approach.

Knowledge management requirements persist across solution types. Open source implementations often require extensive internal knowledge bases and training programs. Proprietary implementations might focus more on platform-specific knowledge and vendor documentation. Organizations must maintain appropriate knowledge management regardless of approach.

Future planning considerations vary between implementation types but remain essential. Open source implementations must consider community direction and internal development capabilities. Proprietary implementations need to align with vendor roadmaps and market evolution. Organizations must establish appropriate planning processes regardless of chosen approach.

Risk management practices differ between solution types but maintain crucial importance. Open source implementations often focus on technical and resource risks. Proprietary implementations might emphasize vendor and cost risks. Organizations must establish appropriate risk management regardless of implementation choice.

Success metrics vary between implementation types but

remain essential for evaluation. Open source implementations might focus on technical performance and customization effectiveness. Proprietary implementations often emphasize business value and user adoption. Organizations must establish appropriate success metrics aligned with their implementation approach.

The selection between open source and proprietary AI solutions requires a structured decision framework that considers multiple factors, capabilities, and organizational requirements. This framework must provide systematic evaluation methods while accommodating unique organizational needs and circumstances.

Evaluation criteria begin with clear assessment of organizational objectives. Technical requirements define necessary capabilities and performance needs. Business requirements establish cost constraints and value expectations. Operational requirements determine support and maintenance needs. These foundational criteria guide initial solution evaluation and selection.

Capability assessment evaluates potential solutions against specific needs. Language AI applications might require specific accuracy levels or processing capabilities. Computer vision solutions need particular recognition capabilities or processing speeds. Data analysis tools must handle specific data types and volumes. Understanding these detailed requirements enables effective solution evaluation.

Resource availability significantly influences solution viability. Technical teams must possess or be able to develop necessary expertise. Infrastructure must support solution requirements. Budget must accommodate total implementation costs. Organizations like Google and Facebook demonstrate how substantial resources enable successful open source implementations, while smaller organizations might benefit from proprietary solutions' managed services.

Technical assessment examines solution architectures and

capabilities. Integration requirements must align with existing systems. Performance capabilities must meet operational needs. Scalability options must support growth expectations. Major cloud providers demonstrate how proprietary solutions can offer comprehensive technical capabilities, while open source frameworks like PyTorch provide extensive technical flexibility.

Cost analysis must consider total implementation expense. Open source solutions eliminate licensing fees but often require significant expertise investment. Proprietary solutions include licensing costs but might reduce technical resource requirements. Cloud platforms demonstrate how usage-based pricing can align costs with value, while open source implementations might require substantial upfront investment.

Risk evaluation examines potential implementation challenges. Technical risks include integration complications and performance issues. Operational risks involve support challenges and maintenance requirements. Strategic risks consider vendor stability or community sustainability. Understanding these risks helps organizations prepare appropriate mitigation strategies.

Timeline considerations influence solution selection. Implementation speed requirements might favor proprietary solutions with established deployment processes. Development flexibility needs might suggest open source approaches. Organizations must align solution choice with schedule requirements and resource availability.

Support requirements significantly impact solution viability. Internal support capabilities must align with chosen solution needs. External support availability must meet organizational requirements. Major vendors demonstrate how proprietary solutions can provide comprehensive support, while open source communities offer collaborative assistance options.

Security requirements influence solution selection

significantly. Internal security capabilities must align with solution needs. External security features must meet organizational standards. Financial institutions demonstrate how security requirements might favor proprietary solutions with established security frameworks, while government agencies might prefer open source solutions enabling thorough security review.

Compliance needs affect solution viability considerably. Regulatory requirements must align with solution capabilities. Audit capabilities must meet organizational standards. Healthcare organizations demonstrate how compliance requirements might influence solution selection, particularly regarding data privacy and protection.

Growth expectations impact solution sustainability. Scaling requirements must align with solution capabilities. Resource availability must support expected growth. Organizations must consider how solution choice affects future expansion possibilities and resource requirements.

Customization needs influence solution suitability. Internal development capabilities must support required modifications. Solution flexibility must enable necessary adaptations. Research institutions demonstrate how customization requirements might favor open source solutions, while commercial enterprises might prefer proprietary solutions' standardized approaches.

Integration requirements affect implementation feasibility. Existing systems must support solution integration. Technical capabilities must enable necessary connections. Organizations must consider how solution choice influences integration complexity and resource requirements.

Operational implications require careful consideration. Management capabilities must align with operational needs. Monitoring requirements must match solution capabilities. Organizations must evaluate how solution choice affects daily operations and maintenance requirements.

Strategic alignment demands thorough evaluation. Long-term objectives must align with solution capabilities. A technology roadmap must support organizational direction. Organizations must consider how solution choice influences strategic flexibility and future opportunities.

Community engagement possibilities influence solution value. Knowledge sharing opportunities must align with organizational needs. Collaboration capabilities must support development requirements. Organizations must evaluate how solution choice affects community participation and knowledge access.

Vendor relationships require careful assessment for proprietary solutions. Support capabilities must meet organizational needs. A development roadmap must align with strategic requirements. Organizations must consider how vendor relationships influence long-term solution success.

Innovation potential affects long-term value. Development flexibility must support innovation needs. Resource availability must enable necessary advancement. Organizations must evaluate how solution choice influences future innovation possibilities.

Success criteria require clear definition and measurement capabilities. Performance metrics must align with organizational objectives. Value measurements must support investment justification. Organizations must establish how solution choice affects success evaluation and reporting capabilities.

Understanding the distinctions between open source and proprietary AI solutions provides essential context for the practical implementations we'll explore throughout this book. The decision framework we've established will prove valuable as we examine specific AI solutions across various domains, beginning with our next chapter's focus on Language AI Solutions.

As we venture into these specific solution domains, we'll encounter both open source and proprietary options. Language AI solutions, for instance, span from open source models enabling complete customization to proprietary services offering immediate capability. We'll see how organizations leverage both approaches, sometimes within the same implementation, to create effective solutions that meet their specific needs.

The principles we've explored regarding licensing, implementation considerations, and decision frameworks apply across all AI solution categories. Whether examining data analysis tools, computer vision systems, or specialized applications, organizations must carefully evaluate their options while considering the factors we've discussed. This foundational understanding enables informed decisions about specific solution implementations.

Our journey continues as we explore these solution categories in detail, beginning with the rapidly evolving field of Language AI. The knowledge we've built about open source and proprietary approaches will illuminate the choices organizations face when implementing these powerful capabilities.

GIL OREN

CHAPTER 4: LANGUAGE AI SOLUTIONS

Having established our understanding of both AI components and implementation approaches, we now turn to one of artificial intelligence's most transformative domains: Language AI. Where previous chapters laid the groundwork for understanding AI solutions broadly, we now examine how these principles apply to systems that process, understand, and generate human language.

The evolution of Language AI represents one of artificial intelligence's most significant achievements. From early rule-based systems to today's sophisticated language models, these solutions have transformed how machines interact with human communication. This progression enables applications ranging from simple text analysis to complex language generation and understanding.

Our exploration of Language AI solutions builds upon the implementation framework established in previous chapters. We'll see how both open source and proprietary approaches shape language processing capabilities, how models and tools combine to create practical solutions, and how platforms support language AI implementation. This practical understanding will illuminate how organizations leverage language AI effectively.

As we begin our examination of specific AI solution categories, Language AI provides an ideal starting point. The principles we uncover here will inform our understanding of other AI domains, while the implementation patterns we explore will reveal common themes in AI solution deployment. Let us examine how Language AI solutions transform theoretical possibilities into practical capabilities.

Natural Language Processing (NLP) forms the foundation of Language AI solutions, enabling machines to interact with human language in meaningful ways. This capability represents one of artificial intelligence's most significant achievements, transforming how machines process, understand, and generate human communication.

The fundamental challenge of language processing lies in bridging the gap between human communication and machine understanding. Where humans naturally grasp context, nuance, and implied meaning, machines must process language through systematic analysis of patterns and relationships. Understanding this challenge helps explain both the capabilities and limitations of current Language AI solutions.

Language AI solutions operate through multiple processing layers, each handling specific aspects of language understanding. Tokenization breaks text into manageable units for processing. Syntactic analysis examines grammatical structures and relationships. Semantic processing determines meaning from these components. Each layer contributes to comprehensive language understanding.

The evolution of Language AI reflects significant technological advancement. Early systems relied on predefined rules and limited pattern matching. Modern solutions employ sophisticated machine learning approaches, enabling more natural language understanding and generation.

This progression demonstrates both the field's rapid development and its continuing challenges.

Consider how Language AI processes text input. The system first breaks down text into tokens, which might represent words, subwords, or characters. These tokens undergo analysis to determine their relationships and roles within the text. The system then applies learned patterns to understand meaning and generate appropriate responses. This systematic processing enables sophisticated language capabilities.

Context plays a crucial role in language understanding. Modern Language AI solutions maintain context awareness through various mechanisms, from attention systems that track relationships between words to memory structures that maintain information across longer sequences. Understanding these context management approaches helps explain both current capabilities and limitations.

The relationship between training data and language processing capabilities shapes solution effectiveness. Models learn language patterns from their training data, influencing their understanding and generation capabilities. This relationship between training and performance helps explain why different solutions excel at different tasks.

Language understanding involves multiple levels of analysis. Surface-level processing examines explicit meaning through word definitions and grammatical structures. Deeper analysis considers implicit meaning, context, and relationships between concepts. Understanding these analysis levels helps guide effective solution implementation.

The generation of human-like text represents another fundamental capability of Language AI. Modern systems can produce coherent, contextually appropriate text by applying learned patterns and relationships. Understanding generation mechanisms helps organizations leverage these capabilities effectively while recognizing their limitations.

Error handling and correction form crucial aspects of

Language AI operation. Systems must manage ambiguous input, incorrect spelling, and grammatical errors. They need to maintain coherent output despite potential input problems. Understanding these error management capabilities helps guide effective implementation.

Multilinguality presents both challenges and opportunities in Language AI. Solutions must handle different language structures, cultural contexts, and communication patterns. Some systems specialize in specific languages while others attempt broader coverage. Understanding these linguistic aspects helps guide solution selection and implementation.

Performance evaluation in Language AI involves multiple criteria. Accuracy measures how well systems understand and process language. Fluency evaluates the naturalness of generated text. Response time assesses processing speed. Understanding these evaluation criteria helps organizations assess solution effectiveness.

The practical impact of Language AI extends throughout modern operations. Customer service applications leverage these capabilities for automated support. Content management systems employ language processing for analysis and generation. Document processing systems extract meaning from unstructured text. Understanding these practical applications helps guide implementation planning.

Resource requirements for Language AI vary significantly between solutions. Some systems demand substantial computational resources for operation. Others optimize for efficiency with more modest requirements. Understanding these resource needs helps organizations plan effective implementations.

The limitations of current Language AI solutions require careful consideration. Systems may struggle with complex context, subtle meaning, or novel situations. They might generate plausible but incorrect information. Understanding these limitations helps organizations implement solutions appropriately.

Integration capabilities significantly influence Language AI effectiveness. Solutions must work with existing systems, handle appropriate data formats, and maintain reliable operation. Understanding integration requirements helps organizations plan successful implementations.

Security considerations play crucial roles in Language AI deployment. Systems must protect sensitive information, maintain appropriate access controls, and prevent misuse. Understanding security requirements helps organizations implement solutions safely.

Privacy management proves particularly important in Language AI implementations. Solutions often process sensitive communications or personal information. They must maintain appropriate data protection while delivering required capabilities. Understanding privacy implications helps guide responsible implementation.

The ongoing evolution of Language AI capabilities continues to expand implementation possibilities. New architectures emerge, training approaches advance, and processing capabilities improve. Understanding this evolution helps organizations plan effective, sustainable implementations.

Development practices for Language AI solutions continue to mature. Best practices emerge for implementation and operation. Standards develop for evaluation and deployment. Understanding these practices helps organizations maintain effective solutions.

The architecture of Language AI models represents sophisticated engineering that enables human language processing. Understanding these architectures proves crucial for effective implementation, providing insight into both capabilities and requirements of different approaches.

Transformer architecture forms the foundation of modern Language AI models. First introduced in 2017, this approach revolutionized natural language processing through its attention mechanisms and parallel processing capabilities.

Understanding transformer architecture helps explain the remarkable capabilities of current language models.

The attention mechanism serves as a crucial component in modern Language AI models. This system enables models to weigh the importance of different words or tokens when processing language. Unlike earlier sequential processing approaches, attention mechanisms consider all parts of the input simultaneously, enabling more sophisticated understanding.

Encoder-decoder structures appear throughout Language AI architectures. Encoders process input text into internal representations, while decoders generate output from these representations. This separation of concerns enables flexible processing while maintaining systematic operation. Understanding these structures helps explain model capabilities and limitations.

Model size significantly influences processing capabilities. Larger models with more parameters often demonstrate more sophisticated language understanding but require substantial computational resources. Smaller models might offer more limited capabilities but operate with greater efficiency. This relationship between size and capability helps guide implementation decisions.

Training approaches significantly affect model capabilities. Supervised learning uses labeled data to teach specific tasks. Unsupervised learning discovers patterns in unlabeled text. Self-supervised learning creates training signals from the text itself. Understanding these training approaches helps explain model behavior and limitations.

Consider how different architectures handle context. Some maintain fixed context windows, limiting the amount of text they can process at once. Others employ mechanisms for handling longer sequences. Advanced architectures might implement sophisticated memory systems for maintaining context across extended interactions. Understanding these context management approaches helps guide implementation planning.

The processing flow within Language AI models follows systematic patterns. Input text undergoes tokenization, converting words or subwords into numerical representations. These tokens flow through multiple processing layers, each contributing to understanding or generation tasks. Output generation reverses this flow, converting internal representations back into human-readable text.

Optimization techniques play crucial roles in model operation. Various approaches balance processing efficiency with output quality. Some architectures implement specialized optimizations for specific tasks or deployment environments. Understanding these optimizations helps organizations plan effective implementations.

Model compression represents an important architectural consideration. Techniques like knowledge distillation, pruning, and quantization can reduce model size while maintaining acceptable performance. These approaches help make sophisticated language processing more accessible across different deployment scenarios.

The handling of special cases requires careful architectural consideration. Models must process unusual inputs, manage edge cases, and maintain reliable operation across varying conditions. Understanding how architectures handle these situations helps guide implementation planning.

Fine-tuning capabilities represent crucial architectural features. Models must support adaptation to specific tasks or domains while maintaining core functionality. Different architectures offer varying approaches to fine-tuning, influencing their suitability for particular applications.

Multilingual support involves specific architectural considerations. Some models implement language-specific components, while others attempt universal language processing. Understanding these approaches helps organizations select appropriate solutions for their language requirements.

Performance optimization features appear throughout model architectures. Caching mechanisms improve response times for common queries. Batching capabilities enable efficient processing of multiple inputs. Understanding these features helps organizations optimize solution performance.

Resource management systems form essential architectural components. Models must efficiently utilize available computing resources while maintaining reliable operation. Different architectures implement varying approaches to resource management, influencing their deployment requirements.

Security features integrate throughout model architectures. Input validation systems protect against malicious content. Output filtering prevents inappropriate generation. Understanding these security features helps organizations implement solutions safely.

The evolution of model architectures continues to advance language processing capabilities. New approaches emerge, existing architectures improve, and implementation options expand. Understanding this evolution helps organizations plan sustainable implementations.

Evaluation frameworks help assess architectural effectiveness. Performance metrics measure processing capabilities. Resource utilization metrics track operational efficiency. Understanding these frameworks helps organizations evaluate potential solutions.

Integration capabilities significantly influence architectural suitability. Models must support appropriate APIs, handle required data formats, and maintain reliable operation within larger systems. Understanding these integration requirements helps guide architecture selection.

The practical impact of architectural decisions extends throughout solution lifecycles. Initial implementation requirements, ongoing operational needs, and future scaling capabilities all depend on architectural choices. Understanding these implications helps organizations plan effective

implementations.

The landscape of core Language AI models represents the practical implementation of architectural principles in functioning systems. Understanding these models, their capabilities, and operational characteristics proves essential for effective solution implementation.

GPT (Generative Pre-trained Transformer) models, developed by OpenAI, demonstrate the evolution of language processing capabilities. Beginning with GPT-1 in 2018, OpenAI established a foundation for large-scale language models. GPT-2, released in 2019, expanded these capabilities significantly, leading to a phased release due to concerns about potential misuse. GPT-3, introduced in 2020, marked a dramatic leap forward with 175 billion parameters, while GPT-4, released in 2023, further advanced these capabilities. Each iteration has expanded processing capabilities while maintaining the fundamental transformer architecture.

BERT (Bidirectional Encoder Representations from Transformers), introduced by Google AI researchers Jacob Devlin, Ming-Wei Chang, Kenton Lee, and Kristina Toutanova in 2018, established crucial advances in language understanding. Their research paper, "BERT: Pre-training of Deep Bidirectional Transformers for Language Understanding," unveiled how bidirectional processing enables sophisticated context understanding by considering text from multiple directions simultaneously. Google's subsequent release of BERT as open source has enabled widespread adoption and innovation.

The T5 (Text-to-Text Transfer Transformer) model, developed by Google Research and introduced in 2019 by Colin Raffel and his team, pioneered a unified approach to language tasks. Published in their paper "Exploring the Limits of Transfer Learning with a Unified Text-to-Text Transformer," T5 introduced the concept of framing every natural language processing task as a text-to-text problem. This approach simplifies implementation while maintaining sophisticated processing capabilities.

Consider how these models handle different processing tasks. OpenAI's GPT models excel at text generation and completion tasks, demonstrating remarkable capabilities in producing coherent, contextually appropriate content. Google's BERT models show particular strength in understanding tasks like question answering and text classification, evidenced by their widespread adoption in search engines and enterprise applications. Google's T5 models demonstrate versatility across various language processing applications through their unified text-to-text approach.

Training data significantly influences model capabilities. GPT models train on vast text collections curated by OpenAI, enabling broad language understanding but potentially incorporating biases. BERT models often undergo specific training for particular domains or languages, with Google and other organizations releasing specialized versions for different applications. Understanding these training influences helps guide model selection and implementation.

Resource requirements vary significantly between models. OpenAI's GPT-4 demands substantial computational resources for operation, while smaller models like DistilBERT, developed by Hugging Face to compress BERT's capabilities, operate effectively with more modest requirements. Understanding these resource needs helps organizations plan appropriate implementations.

Fine-tuning capabilities differ across model types. BERT's architecture enables effective fine-tuning for specific tasks, as demonstrated by numerous domain-specific variants. GPT models offer different approaches to customization, with OpenAI providing various methods for adapting model behavior. Understanding these fine-tuning options helps organizations select appropriate solutions for their needs.

Implementation approaches vary between models. OpenAI provides API access to GPT models through their platform, while BERT and T5 implementations are available through open-source frameworks like Hugging Face's Transformers library. Understanding these implementation requirements helps organizations plan effective solutions.

Performance characteristics show distinct patterns across models. Google's BERT prioritizes understanding accuracy, while OpenAI's GPT models balance generation quality with response time. Understanding these performance characteristics helps guide model selection for specific applications.

Security considerations vary between models. OpenAI implements sophisticated input validation and output filtering for GPT models, while organizations implementing open-source models like BERT must often develop their own security measures. Understanding these security aspects helps organizations implement solutions safely.

Privacy management differs across model types. Open-source models like BERT enable complete local processing control, while API-based services like GPT require external processing. Understanding these privacy implications helps guide appropriate model selection and implementation.

Cost structures vary significantly between models. OpenAI's GPT models require API access payments, while open-source implementations of BERT and T5 need infrastructure investment. Understanding these cost implications helps organizations plan effective implementations.

Integration capabilities differ between models. OpenAI provides comprehensive APIs for GPT integration, while BERT and T5 implementations offer flexible integration through various frameworks. Understanding these integration requirements helps guide implementation planning.

Scalability options vary across model types. Cloud-based services like OpenAI's GPT API handle scaling automatically, while self-hosted models require careful infrastructure planning. Understanding these scalability characteristics helps organizations plan for growth.

Community support varies between models. BERT and T5's open-source nature has fostered extensive community development, while GPT models benefit from OpenAI's dedicated support resources. Understanding these support options helps guide implementation decisions.

Version management differs across models. OpenAI maintains version control for GPT models centrally, while organizations must manage updates for self-hosted BERT or T5 implementations. Understanding these version management aspects helps organizations maintain current capabilities.

Error handling varies between models. Each implementation requires specific approaches to managing input validation, output verification, and error recovery. Understanding these error handling capabilities helps guide effective implementation.

The evolution of these models continues to advance language processing capabilities. Major organizations like OpenAI, Google, and others regularly introduce improvements through new versions and research. Understanding this evolution helps organizations plan sustainable implementations.

The practical impact of model selection extends throughout solution lifecycles. Initial implementation requirements, ongoing operational needs, and future capabilities all depend on model choice. Understanding these implications helps organizations plan effective implementations.

The translation of language AI models into practical tools and applications enables organizations to leverage these capabilities effectively. Understanding the available tools and their implementation approaches proves crucial for successful deployment of language AI solutions.

Development frameworks serve as foundational tools for language AI implementation. The Hugging Face Transformers library, introduced in 2018, provides comprehensive access to numerous pre-trained models and implementation tools. PyTorch and TensorFlow, developed by Facebook and Google respectively, offer robust frameworks for model deployment and customization.

Text analysis tools represent a crucial category of language AI applications. Tools for sentiment analysis examine emotional content in text, while classification systems categorize documents automatically. Named entity recognition tools identify and categorize specific information within text. These capabilities enable automated processing of large text collections.

Content generation tools leverage language models for creative and practical applications. Tools for automated writing assistance help improve text quality and consistency. Marketing content generators create variations of promotional material. Documentation tools help maintain technical information. Understanding these tools' capabilities helps organizations implement appropriate solutions.

Translation services demonstrate practical language AI application. Google Translate, launched in 2006 and significantly enhanced through neural machine translation in 2016, processes numerous languages through sophisticated models. DeepL, introduced in 2017, offers high-quality translation through specialized neural networks. These services demonstrate how language AI enables practical communication solutions.

Question answering systems showcase interactive language AI capabilities. Tools can process natural language queries and extract relevant information from documents. Some systems maintain context through conversations, enabling more natural interaction. Understanding these capabilities helps organizations implement effective information access solutions.

Document processing tools apply language AI to business operations. Systems for information extraction identify key data in documents automatically. Classification tools organize documents by content and purpose. These capabilities enable efficient handling of large document collections.

Communication tools leverage language AI for various interactions. Customer service chatbots provide automated response capabilities. Email processing systems help manage communication flow. Meeting transcription services convert spoken language to text automatically. These applications demonstrate practical language AI implementation.

Integration tools enable connection between language AI and existing systems. API management tools handle communication with language services. Data transformation tools prepare information for processing. Results management tools handle system outputs. Understanding these integration capabilities helps organizations implement effective solutions.

Development environments support language AI implementation. Jupyter notebooks enable interactive development and testing. Integrated development environments provide comprehensive tool access. Cloud platforms offer development and deployment capabilities. These environments help organizations create and maintain language AI solutions.

Testing tools ensure reliable solution operation. Validation systems verify processing accuracy. Performance testing tools measure response times and resource usage. Security testing ensures appropriate protection measures. Understanding these testing capabilities helps organizations maintain reliable solutions.

Monitoring tools track operational performance. Usage monitoring measures system activity and resource consumption. Quality monitoring verifies processing accuracy. Security monitoring tracks potential issues. These capabilities help organizations maintain effective operations.

Management tools support ongoing operation. Version control systems track solution changes. Configuration management maintains system settings. Resource management optimizes system operation. Understanding these management capabilities helps organizations maintain effective solutions.

Security tools protect language AI implementations. Input validation prevents harmful content processing. Output filtering ensures appropriate responses. Access control manages system usage. These capabilities help organizations maintain secure operations.

Optimization tools improve solution performance. Caching systems speed response times for common queries. Load balancing distributes processing effectively. Resource management ensures efficient operation. Understanding these optimization capabilities helps organizations maintain effective solutions.

Analytics tools measure solution effectiveness. Usage analytics track system activity patterns. Performance analytics measure processing efficiency. Quality analytics verify output accuracy. These capabilities help organizations evaluate and improve operations.

Deployment tools support solution implementation. Container systems enable consistent deployment. Orchestration tools manage system operation. Scaling tools handle growing requirements. Understanding these deployment capabilities helps organizations implement effective solutions.

Documentation tools support solution maintenance. API documentation describes integration capabilities. Operation guides explain system management. User guides support effective usage. These resources help organizations maintain solution knowledge.

Training tools support user preparation. Tutorial systems explain solution capabilities. Practice environments enable safe learning. Reference materials provide ongoing support. These resources help organizations prepare for effective solution usage.

Support tools assist with ongoing operation. Problem

tracking systems manage issue resolution. Knowledge bases provide solution information. Communication systems enable assistance access. These capabilities help organizations maintain effective operations.

The successful deployment of Language AI solutions requires careful attention to numerous implementation factors. Beyond selecting appropriate models and tools, organizations must consider various operational, technical, and practical aspects that influence implementation success.

Resource planning forms a crucial foundation for Language AI implementation. Computational requirements vary significantly between solutions, from cloud-based services requiring minimal local resources to self-hosted models demanding substantial computing power. Organizations must evaluate their existing infrastructure, determine additional needs, and plan for appropriate resource allocation.

Technical expertise requirements significantly influence implementation success. Organizations need team members who understand language processing concepts, machine learning principles, and practical deployment considerations. Skills ranging from model selection and configuration to integration development and performance optimization prove essential for effective implementation.

Integration planning determines how Language AI solutions connect with existing systems. Data flow patterns must accommodate language processing requirements. API implementations need appropriate security and performance characteristics. Database connections require efficient operation. Understanding these integration needs helps organizations plan effective implementations.

Performance management ensures reliable solution operation. Response time requirements influence model and deployment choices. Resource utilization needs careful monitoring and optimization. Scaling capabilities must match organizational growth expectations. These performance considerations shape implementation decisions and ongoing operations.

Security requirements demand careful attention throughout implementation. Input validation prevents harmful content processing. Access control protects system resources. Data protection ensures appropriate information handling. Organizations must implement comprehensive security measures while maintaining efficient operation.

Privacy considerations significantly influence implementation approaches. Data handling procedures must protect sensitive information. Processing locations need careful evaluation. Access controls require appropriate restrictions. Organizations must balance privacy requirements with operational needs.

Compliance requirements affect numerous implementation aspects. Data protection regulations influence processing approaches. Industry standards affect security measures. Documentation needs reflect compliance obligations. Organizations must ensure implementations meet all relevant requirements.

Cost management extends beyond initial implementation expenses. Ongoing operational costs require careful evaluation. Support and maintenance expenses need consideration. Growth costs must factor into planning. Understanding total cost implications helps organizations plan sustainable implementations.

Training requirements affect implementation success significantly. Users need appropriate preparation for effective system usage. Support staff require operational knowledge. Development teams need implementation expertise. Organizations must plan appropriate training throughout implementation.

Documentation needs span multiple areas. Technical documentation supports implementation and maintenance. User documentation enables effective system usage. Operational documentation guides ongoing management.

Organizations must maintain appropriate documentation throughout implementation.

Testing requirements ensure reliable operation. Functional testing verifies basic capabilities. Performance testing confirms operational characteristics. Security testing validates protection measures. Organizations must implement comprehensive testing throughout solution lifecycle.

Monitoring needs support ongoing operation. Performance monitoring tracks system behavior. Security monitoring identifies potential issues. Usage monitoring guides optimization efforts. Organizations must implement appropriate monitoring capabilities.

Maintenance planning ensures continued effective operation. Regular updates maintain current capabilities. Performance optimization improves operation. Security management ensures ongoing protection. Organizations must plan appropriate maintenance throughout solution lifecycle.

Scaling considerations affect long-term success. Growth requirements influence initial implementation. Resource planning must accommodate expansion. Performance characteristics need appropriate scaling capabilities. Organizations must plan for growth throughout implementation.

Support requirements ensure reliable operation. Technical support helps resolve issues. User support assists with system usage. Development support aids implementation efforts. Organizations must plan appropriate support throughout solution lifecycle.

Version management maintains solution currency. Update procedures keep systems current. Testing processes verify changes. Rollback capabilities ensure reliability. Organizations must manage versions effectively throughout implementation.

Integration management ensures reliable system connection. API management maintains stable interfaces. Data flow management ensures efficient operation. Error handling provides reliable recovery. Organizations must manage integration effectively throughout implementation.

Disaster recovery planning ensures operational continuity. Backup procedures protect essential data. Recovery processes restore operation. Testing validates capabilities. Organizations must plan appropriate recovery throughout implementation.

Risk management addresses potential issues. Technical risks require appropriate mitigation. Operational risks need careful management. Strategic risks demand appropriate planning. Organizations must manage risks effectively throughout implementation.

The practical applications of Language AI solutions demonstrate their transformative impact across various domains. Understanding these applications helps organizations identify implementation opportunities while providing concrete examples of successful deployment.

Text analysis applications process written content for various purposes. Financial institutions analyze market reports and news to inform investment decisions. Healthcare organizations examine medical literature and patient records to support clinical decisions. Legal firms process case documents and regulations to assist research efforts. These applications demonstrate how Language AI enables efficient information processing.

Content generation serves numerous business needs. Marketing departments generate initial drafts of promotional materials, saving time while maintaining consistency. Technical teams create documentation drafts, accelerating documentation processes. News organizations generate preliminary reports from structured data. These applications showcase Language AI's ability to assist with content creation while requiring appropriate human oversight.

Translation services support global operations. International businesses use Language AI to facilitate communication across language barriers. Academic institutions translate research materials to broaden access. Government agencies process multilingual documents for various purposes. These applications demonstrate how Language AI enables effective cross-language communication.

Customer service applications leverage conversational capabilities. Companies implement chatbots for initial customer interaction, routing complex issues to human agents. Support systems analyze customer inquiries to suggest appropriate responses. Service management systems process and categorize customer feedback. These applications show how Language AI enhances customer interaction while maintaining appropriate human involvement.

Document processing handles various content types. Insurance companies process claims documentation to extract relevant information. Healthcare providers analyze medical records to support patient care. Legal firms examine contracts to identify key terms and conditions. These applications demonstrate Language AI's ability to process complex documents effectively.

Research applications assist with information discovery. Scientists use Language AI to analyze research papers and identify relevant studies. Market researchers process consumer feedback to identify trends. Academic institutions analyze student work to provide feedback. These applications show how Language AI supports research and analysis tasks.

Educational applications support learning processes. Educational institutions use Language AI to provide writing feedback to students. Training systems offer interactive learning experiences. Assessment tools help evaluate student work. These applications demonstrate how Language AI supports educational objectives while maintaining appropriate educational standards.

Healthcare applications assist medical professionals. Systems analyze patient records to identify potential issues. Documentation tools help maintain accurate records. Research systems process medical literature to support clinical decisions. These applications show how Language AI supports healthcare delivery while maintaining appropriate medical oversight.

Financial applications process market information. Trading systems analyze news and reports to identify market trends. Risk management systems examine financial documents to identify potential issues. Compliance systems process regulations to ensure adherence. These applications demonstrate how Language AI supports financial operations while maintaining appropriate controls.

Legal applications assist with document processing. Law firms analyze case documents to identify relevant precedents. Contract systems examine agreements to identify key terms. Compliance systems process regulations to ensure adherence. These applications show how Language AI supports legal work while maintaining appropriate professional standards.

Manufacturing applications support operations. Quality systems process production documentation to identify potential issues. Maintenance systems analyze equipment records to predict needs. Safety systems process incident reports to identify trends. These applications demonstrate how Language AI supports manufacturing processes.

Retail applications enhance customer interaction. Product recommendation systems analyze customer behavior to suggest items. Review analysis systems process customer feedback to identify trends. Marketing systems generate promotional content for various channels. These applications show how Language AI supports retail operations.

Media applications assist with content management. News organizations use Language AI to categorize and summarize articles. Entertainment companies process viewer feedback to identify preferences. Publishing houses analyze manuscripts to assess market potential. These applications demonstrate how Language AI supports media operations.

Government applications process public information. Agencies analyze public feedback on proposed regulations. Service systems process citizen inquiries to provide appropriate responses. Documentation systems maintain public records. These applications show how Language AI supports government operations while maintaining appropriate oversight.

Scientific applications assist research efforts. Researchers analyze scientific literature to identify relevant studies. Laboratory systems process experimental data to identify patterns. Publication systems assist with documentation. These applications demonstrate how Language AI supports scientific research.

Technology applications support development efforts. Development teams use Language AI to analyze code and suggest improvements. Documentation systems maintain technical information. Support systems process user inquiries to provide assistance. These applications show how Language AI supports technology development.

Security applications monitor communication patterns. Systems analyze communication flows to identify potential issues. Threat assessment tools process security information to identify risks. Response systems assist with incident management. These applications demonstrate how Language AI supports security operations.

Human resources applications assist with personnel management. Recruitment systems process job applications to identify candidates. Training systems provide interactive learning experiences. Performance systems analyze feedback to identify trends. These applications show how Language AI supports human resource management.

Project management applications enhance coordination. Systems analyze project documentation to identify potential issues. Communication tools process team interaction to enhance collaboration. Planning systems assist with resource allocation. These applications demonstrate how Language AI supports project management while maintaining appropriate human oversight.

The future of Language AI solutions continues to evolve through technological advancement and expanding implementation possibilities. Understanding emerging trends and potential developments helps organizations prepare for future capabilities while planning current implementations.

The evolution of model architecture promises enhanced processing capabilities. Research into more efficient attention mechanisms may enable better performance with reduced computational requirements. Advances in context handling could expand the scope of language understanding. These architectural developments may create new implementation possibilities while improving existing capabilities.

Multimodal processing represents a significant development direction. The integration of language processing with vision, audio, and other modalities enables more comprehensive understanding. OpenAI's GPT-4V (formerly GPT-4 Vision) demonstrates this trend through its ability to process both text and images. These capabilities suggest future applications combining multiple forms of communication.

Efficiency improvements continue to advance implementation possibilities. Techniques for model compression and optimization enable broader deployment options. Research into more efficient training methods may reduce development requirements. These advances could make sophisticated language processing more accessible across different scenarios.

Specialized models are emerging for particular domains. Healthcare-specific language models incorporate medical knowledge for improved accuracy. Financial models integrate domain expertise for better analysis. These specialized solutions suggest increasing adaptation of language processing for specific applications.

Implementation tools are continuously evolving and improving. Development frameworks add capabilities for easier deployment. Management tools enhance operational control. Integration tools simplify system connection. These improvements may make Language AI implementation more accessible while maintaining sophisticated capabilities.

Privacy-preserving techniques are advancing protection capabilities. Local processing options reduce data exposure risks. Encrypted computation methods enable secure processing. These developments may enhance privacy protection while maintaining processing capabilities.

Regulatory frameworks continue to evolve around Language AI. Data protection requirements influence implementation approaches. Ethical guidelines shape development practices. These regulatory developments may affect how organizations implement and operate Language AI solutions.

Resource requirements are trending toward greater efficiency. Optimization techniques reduce computational needs. Deployment options expand for different scenarios. These efficiency improvements may make sophisticated language processing more widely accessible.

Integration capabilities continue to expand. New protocols enable better system connection. Standards development improves interoperability. These advances may simplify how organizations implement Language AI within existing operations.

User interaction methods are becoming more sophisticated. Natural language interfaces improve system accessibility. Multimodal interaction enables more intuitive operation. These developments may enhance how users engage with Language AI solutions.

Quality improvement techniques are advancing solution reliability. Better evaluation methods enable more accurate assessment. Enhanced testing approaches improve validation. These advances may improve how organizations ensure solution effectiveness.

Security measures continue to evolve. New protection methods address emerging threats. Enhanced monitoring improves issue detection. These security developments may improve how organizations protect Language AI

implementations.

Ethical considerations are gaining increasing attention. Bias detection methods improve fairness. Transparency tools enhance understanding. These developments may influence how organizations implement and operate Language AI solutions.

Implementation practices continue to mature. Best practices evolve from experience. Standards develop for different scenarios. These developments may improve how organizations approach Language AI implementation.

Cost structures evolve with technology advancement. New deployment options affect expenses. Efficiency improvements influence operational costs. These developments may change how organizations plan Language AI implementations.

Support systems are becoming more sophisticated. Automated assistance improves issue resolution. Knowledge management enhances information access. These advances may improve how organizations maintain Language AI solutions.

Performance optimization continues to advance. New techniques improve processing efficiency. Better monitoring enables optimization. These developments may enhance how organizations operate Language AI solutions.

Integration patterns evolve with experience. New approaches simplify system connection. Standards improve interoperability. These advances may improve how organizations implement Language AI within existing systems.

The future of Language AI suggests continuing evolution in capabilities, implementation approaches, and operational practices. Organizations must maintain awareness of these developments while planning current implementations to ensure sustainable, effective solutions.

Our exploration of Language AI solutions has revealed the practical implementation possibilities of these transformative technologies. From understanding fundamental architectures to examining specific tools and applications, we've built a comprehensive foundation for implementing language processing capabilities effectively.

This understanding of Language AI prepares us for examining another crucial domain of artificial intelligence: Data AI solutions. While language processing enables machines to understand and generate human communication, data analysis allows organizations to extract meaningful insights from vast information collections. Many organizations implement both capabilities, using Language AI to process unstructured text while leveraging Data AI to analyze structured information.

The principles we've explored regarding model selection, implementation considerations, and practical applications apply similarly to data analysis solutions. The careful evaluation of requirements, thorough implementation planning, and attention to operational considerations remain crucial for successful deployment.

As we move forward to examine Data AI solutions, we'll see how different analytical approaches enable organizations to understand patterns, predict trends, and make informed decisions. The journey continues as we explore how these capabilities transform raw data into actionable intelligence.

CHAPTER 5: DATA AI SOLUTIONS

Having explored the realm of Language AI solutions, we now turn our attention to another fundamental domain of artificial intelligence: Data AI solutions. Where language processing enables understanding of human communication, data analysis empowers organizations to extract meaningful insights from vast collections of information, transforming raw data into actionable intelligence.

The evolution of Data AI reflects the exponential growth in available information across all sectors. Organizations now generate and collect unprecedented volumes of data, from transaction records and sensor readings to customer interactions and operational metrics. This abundance of information creates both opportunities and challenges, driving the development of sophisticated analytical solutions.

Our journey through Data AI solutions will examine how organizations leverage various models, tools, and platforms to process this information effectively. From gradient boosting frameworks like XGBoost and LightGBM to comprehensive platforms like Databricks, we'll explore how different approaches enable sophisticated data analysis while maintaining practical implementation focus.

The relationship between Data AI and other AI domains proves particularly significant. While Language AI processes unstructured text and Audio/Vision AI handles rich media content, Data AI solutions often work alongside these technologies, analyzing their outputs while providing additional insights through structured data analysis. Understanding these relationships helps organizations implement comprehensive AI strategies.

As we begin our exploration of Data AI solutions, we'll maintain our focus on practical implementation while ensuring thorough understanding of fundamental concepts. The journey ahead reveals how organizations transform data from a passive resource into a dynamic driver of decision-making and innovation.

Data AI solutions represent the systematic application of artificial intelligence to information analysis and interpretation. Understanding these fundamentals proves essential for effective implementation, providing context for how different approaches transform raw data into valuable insights.

The foundation of Data AI begins with understanding different data types. Structured data follows predefined formats, like database records or spreadsheet entries, enabling direct analysis through statistical methods. Unstructured data, including text documents, images, and sensor readings, requires preprocessing before analysis. Semi-structured data combines elements of both, requiring flexible processing approaches.

Data processing forms a crucial component of analytics workflows. Extract, Transform, Load (ETL) processes, first developed in the 1970s and continuously evolved, prepare data for analysis. Modern ELT (Extract, Load, Transform) approaches, enabled by increased computing power, offer alternative workflows. Understanding these processing approaches helps organizations plan effective

implementations.

Statistical analysis provides essential foundations for Data AI. Descriptive statistics summarize data characteristics, while inferential statistics enable conclusions about larger populations. Probability theory underlies many analytical methods, from basic forecasting to sophisticated machine learning models. These mathematical foundations enable reliable analysis and interpretation.

Machine learning approaches significantly enhance analytical capabilities. Supervised learning uses labeled data to develop predictive models. Unsupervised learning discovers patterns without predefined categories. Reinforcement learning enables systems to improve through interaction with data. Understanding these approaches helps guide appropriate method selection.

Feature engineering plays a crucial role in data preparation. This process transforms raw data into formats suitable for analysis, creating new variables that better represent underlying patterns. The quality of feature engineering significantly influences analytical results, making it a crucial skill for effective implementation.

Dimensionality considerations significantly affect analysis approaches. High-dimensional data, containing many variables, presents specific challenges for processing and interpretation. Dimension reduction techniques help manage complexity while maintaining important information. Understanding these considerations helps guide appropriate method selection.

Data quality management ensures reliable analysis results. Validation procedures verify data accuracy and completeness. Cleaning processes address inconsistencies and errors. Quality metrics track data reliability over time. These practices help maintain effective analytical operations.

Scale considerations influence processing approaches. Big data environments require distributed processing capabilities. Real-time analysis demands efficient processing methods.

Batch processing enables systematic handling of large data volumes. Understanding these scaling factors helps guide implementation planning.

Time series analysis represents a crucial analytical domain. These methods examine data patterns over time, enabling trend identification and forecasting. Different approaches handle various temporal patterns, from simple trends to complex seasonal variations. Understanding these methods helps organizations leverage historical data effectively.

Optimization techniques improve analytical efficiency. Algorithm selection matches processing methods to data characteristics. Parameter tuning enhances model performance. Resource allocation ensures efficient processing. These optimization approaches help maintain effective operations.

Visualization plays an essential role in data understanding. Different visualization types serve various analytical needs, from simple trend display to complex pattern representation. Interactive visualizations enable detailed data exploration. Understanding visualization approaches helps communicate insights effectively.

Model evaluation ensures reliable analytical results. Validation methods verify model performance. Testing procedures confirm processing reliability. Performance metrics track operational effectiveness. These evaluation practices help maintain solution quality.

Integration considerations affect implementation success. Data sources require appropriate connection methods. Processing systems need efficient interaction. Results delivery demands reliable distribution. Understanding these integration needs helps guide effective implementation.

Security requirements demand careful attention. Access controls protect sensitive data. Encryption safeguards information during processing. Audit trails track system usage. These security measures help maintain appropriate protection.

Privacy considerations significantly influence

implementation. Data anonymization protects individual information. Processing controls prevent unauthorized access. Result filtering ensures appropriate information sharing. These privacy practices help maintain regulatory compliance.

Performance optimization ensures efficient operation. Processing efficiency reduces resource requirements. Response time optimization improves user experience. Resource management ensures sustainable operation. These optimization practices help maintain effective solutions.

Scalability planning supports growing requirements. Infrastructure design accommodates increased processing needs. Resource allocation adapts to changing demands. Performance monitoring guides scaling decisions. These planning practices help maintain sustainable operations.

Error handling ensures reliable processing. Data validation catches input issues. Processing monitoring identifies operational problems. Recovery procedures address system issues. These error management practices help maintain reliable operation.

Maintenance requirements ensure ongoing effectiveness. Regular updates maintain current capabilities. Performance optimization improves operation. Security management ensures continued protection. These maintenance practices help sustain effective solutions.

Core Data AI models provide the analytical engines that power modern data processing and analysis solutions. Understanding these models, their capabilities, and implementation considerations proves essential for effective solution deployment.

XGBoost (eXtreme Gradient Boosting), developed by Tianqi Chen and released in 2014, represents a significant advancement in gradient boosting frameworks. This open-source model combines sophisticated optimization techniques with efficient processing methods, enabling high-performance analysis of structured data. Initially developed during Chen's Ph.D. research at the University of Washington, XGBoost has become a standard tool in data science competitions and enterprise implementations.

The fundamental architecture of XGBoost builds upon gradient boosting principles. The system creates an ensemble of decision trees, each addressing errors from previous trees. Novel techniques like parallel processing and cache-aware computation enable efficient operation on large datasets. Understanding these architectural elements helps guide effective implementation.

LightGBM, developed by Microsoft Research and released in 2017, offers another powerful gradient boosting framework. Its Gradient-based One-Side Sampling (GOSS) and Exclusive Feature Bundling (EFB) techniques enable efficient processing of large datasets. These innovations reduce memory usage while maintaining analytical accuracy, making it particularly valuable for large-scale applications.

TensorFlow, while primarily known for deep learning, provides sophisticated capabilities for data analysis. Developed by the Google Brain team and released as open source in 2015, TensorFlow's flexible architecture enables implementation of various analytical approaches. Its automatic differentiation and optimization capabilities support both traditional analysis and advanced machine learning applications.

Model selection requires careful consideration of various factors. XGBoost typically excels at structured data analysis, particularly for tabular data with clear feature relationships. LightGBM often provides faster processing for large datasets, though with different memory usage patterns. TensorFlow offers flexibility for complex analytical needs, especially when combining traditional analysis with deep learning approaches.

Implementation approaches vary between models. XGBoost provides comprehensive APIs for multiple programming languages, enabling flexible integration. LightGBM offers efficient implementation options, particularly for distributed processing environments.

TensorFlow's ecosystem provides extensive tools for model development and deployment.

Performance characteristics differ significantly between models. XGBoost typically provides excellent accuracy but may require more memory for large datasets. LightGBM often operates more efficiently with large data volumes but might require careful parameter tuning. TensorFlow's performance varies based on implementation approach and hardware utilization.

Resource requirements vary between implementations. XGBoost's tree-based approach requires sufficient memory for tree construction and optimization. LightGBM's efficient memory usage enables processing of larger datasets with limited resources. TensorFlow's requirements depend significantly on implementation architecture and processing approach.

Optimization capabilities differ between models. XGBoost includes sophisticated regularization options for preventing overfitting. LightGBM provides various parameters for tuning processing efficiency and model accuracy. TensorFlow offers extensive optimization options through its computational graph architecture.

Integration considerations affect implementation success. XGBoost provides native integration with many data science frameworks. LightGBM offers efficient integration options for distributed processing environments. TensorFlow's extensive ecosystem enables various integration approaches.

Scaling characteristics influence deployment options. XGBoost supports distributed processing through various frameworks. LightGBM's efficient design enables effective scaling on limited resources. TensorFlow provides extensive options for distributed and parallel processing.

Development practices vary between models. XGBoost's mature ecosystem provides extensive documentation and implementation examples. LightGBM's growing community offers increasing resources for development. TensorFlow's comprehensive documentation supports various implementation approaches.

Security considerations require careful attention. Model protection prevents unauthorized access or modification. Data security ensures appropriate information protection during processing. Implementation security maintains system integrity.

Version management affects ongoing operation. XGBoost maintains regular release cycles with clear upgrade paths. LightGBM provides systematic version updates with compatibility considerations. TensorFlow's versioning system supports stable implementations while enabling access to new features.

Documentation requirements support effective implementation. Technical documentation explains model operation and configuration. Integration documentation guides system connection. Operation documentation supports ongoing management.

Community support varies between models. XGBoost's extensive community provides implementation guidance and problem resolution. LightGBM's growing community offers increasing support resources. TensorFlow's large community supports various implementation approaches.

Error handling capabilities differ between implementations. XGBoost provides comprehensive error detection and reporting. LightGBM includes various monitoring and debugging capabilities. TensorFlow offers extensive tools for tracking and resolving issues.

Performance monitoring ensures reliable operation. Processing efficiency tracking guides optimization efforts. Resource utilization monitoring ensures efficient operation. Quality metrics verify analytical accuracy.

Future development continues across all models. New capabilities emerge through ongoing research and development. Implementation options expand with growing community contributions. These developments create new possibilities while requiring attention to version management.

Data analysis tools transform theoretical capabilities into practical solutions, enabling organizations to implement sophisticated analytical capabilities effectively. Understanding these tools, their capabilities, and implementation considerations proves essential for successful deployment.

Tableau, founded in 2003 at Stanford University and later acquired by Salesforce in 2019, represents a leading solution in data visualization and business intelligence. The platform enables interactive data exploration and visualization through an intuitive interface while supporting connection to various data sources. Its VizQL technology, developed by Pat Hanrahan, Chris Stolte, and Christian Chabot, fundamentally changed how organizations interact with data.

Business intelligence platforms provide comprehensive analytical capabilities. Tableau's interactive dashboards enable real-time data exploration and analysis. Power BI, developed by Microsoft and released in 2014, offers extensive integration with Microsoft's ecosystem. Looker, acquired by Google in 2020, provides sophisticated data modeling and analysis capabilities. Understanding these platforms helps organizations select appropriate solutions for their needs.

DataRobot, founded in 2012, pioneered automated machine learning (AutoML) platforms. The system automates various aspects of the machine learning lifecycle, from data preparation to model deployment. Its automated approach enables organizations to implement sophisticated analysis without requiring extensive data science expertise, though understanding fundamental principles remains crucial for effective implementation.

The Databricks Lakehouse Platform, developed by the original creators of Apache Spark, combines data warehousing with data lake flexibility. Released in 2013, the platform enables unified analytics, combining SQL, streaming, and machine learning capabilities. Its architectural approach supports both traditional structured analysis and modern big data processing needs.

Data preparation tools support effective analysis. Alteryx, founded in 1997, provides workflows for data cleaning and preparation. Trifacta, released in 2012, offers data wrangling capabilities through an interactive interface. These tools enable efficient data preparation while maintaining data quality.

Visualization capabilities vary between tools. Tableau excels at interactive visualization through its drag-and-drop interface. Power BI provides extensive visualization options with Microsoft Office integration. Looker offers sophisticated visualization capabilities through its modeling language.

Integration capabilities significantly influence tool selection. Tableau provides numerous data connectors for various sources. Power BI offers extensive integration within the Microsoft ecosystem. Databricks enables connection to various data sources while maintaining processing efficiency.

Performance optimization varies between implementations. Tableau implements sophisticated caching for interactive performance. Power BI provides various optimization options for large datasets. Databricks offers extensive performance tuning capabilities through its Spark-based architecture.

Security features protect analytical operations. Role-based access controls restrict data and functionality access. Encryption protects sensitive information during processing. Audit trails track system usage and modifications.

Scalability characteristics influence deployment options. Tableau Server enables enterprise-wide deployment and collaboration. Power BI Premium provides dedicated resources for larger implementations. Databricks offers cloud-based scaling capabilities for varying workloads.

Cost structures vary significantly between tools. Tableau offers various licensing options for different deployment scales. Power BI provides different tiers of functionality and capacity. Databricks implements usage-based pricing for cloud resources.

Support options differ between platforms. Tableau maintains extensive documentation and community resources. Power BI provides Microsoft enterprise support options. DataRobot offers dedicated support for AutoML implementations.

Development capabilities support solution customization. Tableau offers extensive customization through calculated fields and parameters. Power BI enables custom visualization development. Databricks supports custom code implementation through notebooks.

Version management ensures reliable operation. Regular updates maintain current capabilities while introducing new features. Compatibility management ensures consistent operation across versions. Update planning prevents operational disruption.

Documentation requirements support effective implementation. Technical documentation explains tool capabilities and configuration. Integration documentation guides system connection. Operation documentation supports ongoing management.

Training resources enable effective tool usage. Official certification programs verify user expertise. Online tutorials provide implementation guidance. Community resources share implementation experiences.

Error handling capabilities maintain reliable operation. Input validation prevents processing issues. Error detection identifies operational problems. Recovery procedures address system issues.

Performance monitoring ensures efficient operation. Usage tracking guides resource allocation. Performance metrics identify optimization needs. Quality measures verify analytical accuracy.

Implementation planning supports successful deployment. Resource requirements guide infrastructure planning. Integration needs influence system design. Security considerations shape implementation approach.

The evolution of these tools continues through regular development. New capabilities emerge from ongoing research. Implementation options expand with growing experience. These developments create new possibilities while requiring careful version management.

The successful implementation of Data AI solutions requires careful attention to numerous operational, technical, and organizational factors. Understanding these considerations helps ensure effective solution deployment while maintaining reliable operation.

Resource planning begins with infrastructure assessment. Computing requirements vary significantly between solutions, from cloud-based services requiring minimal local resources to on-premises implementations demanding substantial computing power. Storage needs range from basic databases to distributed data lakes. Network capabilities must support data movement and processing requirements.

Data management forms a crucial foundation for successful implementation. Data quality procedures ensure accurate analysis through validation and cleaning processes. Data governance establishes rules for information handling and usage. Data lifecycle management guides storage and retention decisions. These considerations significantly influence implementation success.

Technical expertise requirements vary based on implementation approach. Data engineers manage information flow and storage. Data scientists develop and optimize analytical models. Business analysts interpret results and guide implementation. Understanding these expertise needs helps organizations prepare appropriate teams.

Security implementation demands comprehensive protection measures. Access controls restrict system and data usage to authorized users. Encryption protects information during storage and processing. Audit trails track system activity and changes. These security measures help maintain appropriate protection while enabling effective operation.

Integration planning ensures reliable system connection. API implementation enables systematic data exchange. Workflow integration maintains efficient operation. Error handling provides reliable recovery from issues. These integration considerations help create effective solutions.

Performance management ensures reliable operation. Response time requirements influence implementation decisions. Resource utilization needs careful monitoring and optimization. Scaling capabilities must match organizational growth expectations. Understanding these performance factors helps guide implementation planning.

Cost management extends beyond initial implementation expenses. Infrastructure costs include computing, storage, and network resources. Licensing fees vary between solutions and deployment scales. Operational expenses include maintenance, support, and training needs. Understanding total cost implications helps organizations plan sustainable implementations.

Compliance requirements significantly influence implementation approaches. Data protection regulations affect processing methods and storage locations. Industry standards guide security measures and operational procedures. Documentation requirements ensure appropriate record keeping. These compliance considerations help maintain regulatory alignment.

Training requirements affect implementation success. Users need appropriate preparation for effective system usage. Administrators require operational knowledge for system management. Developers need implementation expertise for solution maintenance. Understanding these training needs helps organizations prepare for effective operation.

Change management supports successful implementation. Process changes require careful planning and communication. User adoption needs appropriate support and encouragement. Organization alignment ensures effective solution usage.

These change management considerations help ensure implementation success.

Documentation needs span multiple areas. Technical documentation supports implementation and maintenance. User documentation enables effective system usage. Operational documentation guides ongoing management. These documentation requirements help maintain solution knowledge and capability.

Testing requirements ensure reliable operation. Functional testing verifies basic capabilities. Performance testing confirms operational characteristics. Security testing validates protection measures. These testing considerations help maintain reliable solutions.

Monitoring needs support ongoing operation. Performance monitoring tracks system behavior. Security monitoring identifies potential issues. Usage monitoring guides optimization efforts. These monitoring capabilities help maintain effective operation.

Disaster recovery planning ensures operational continuity. Backup procedures protect essential data and configurations. Recovery processes restore operation after issues. Testing validates recovery capabilities. These planning considerations help maintain reliable operation.

Version management maintains solution currency. Update procedures keep systems current. Testing processes verify changes. Rollback capabilities ensure reliability. These version management considerations help maintain effective solutions.

Scaling considerations affect long-term success. Growth requirements influence initial implementation. Resource planning must accommodate expansion. Performance characteristics need appropriate scaling capabilities. These scaling considerations help ensure sustainable operation.

Support requirements ensure reliable operation. Technical support helps resolve issues. User support assists with system usage. Development support aids implementation efforts. These support considerations help maintain effective solutions.

Quality management ensures reliable results. Validation procedures verify processing accuracy. Testing confirms operational reliability. Monitoring tracks ongoing performance. These quality considerations help maintain effective solutions.

Risk management addresses potential issues. Technical risks require appropriate mitigation. Operational risks need careful management. Strategic risks demand appropriate planning. These risk management considerations help maintain reliable operation.

Future planning ensures sustainable implementation. Technology evolution requires ongoing attention. Capability needs continue to develop. Integration requirements evolve over time. These planning considerations help maintain effective solutions.

The practical applications of Data AI solutions demonstrate their transformative impact across industries and functions. Understanding these applications helps organizations identify implementation opportunities while providing concrete examples of successful deployment.

Business intelligence applications represent a fundamental use case for Data AI. Organizations implement dashboard solutions using tools like Tableau or Power BI to monitor key performance indicators. Sales analysis systems track revenue patterns and customer behavior. Financial reporting tools provide real-time insight into operational performance. These applications enable data-driven decision-making throughout organizations.

Predictive analytics applications leverage historical data to forecast future trends. Retail organizations predict inventory requirements based on sales patterns and seasonal factors. Financial institutions forecast market movements using economic indicators and historical data. Manufacturing companies predict maintenance needs through equipment performance analysis. These applications help organizations prepare for future scenarios effectively.

Customer analytics applications provide insight into consumer behavior. E-commerce platforms analyze purchase patterns to recommend products. Service organizations examine customer interaction data to improve experiences. Marketing teams analyze campaign performance to optimize strategies. These applications help organizations understand and serve their customers more effectively.

Supply chain applications optimize operational efficiency. Inventory management systems predict stock requirements and optimize ordering. Logistics applications optimize delivery routes and timing. Supplier management systems analyze performance and reliability. These applications help organizations maintain efficient operations while reducing costs.

Financial applications support various analytical needs. Risk management systems analyze transaction patterns to identify potential fraud. Investment analysis tools evaluate market conditions and opportunities. Budget planning systems forecast financial requirements and track performance. These applications help organizations manage financial operations effectively.

Healthcare applications leverage data for improved patient care. Diagnostic systems analyze patient data to identify potential issues. Treatment planning tools examine effectiveness patterns. Resource management systems optimize facility utilization. These applications help healthcare providers deliver effective care while managing costs.

Manufacturing applications optimize production processes. Quality control systems analyze production data to identify issues. Process optimization tools identify efficiency improvements. Resource planning systems manage production requirements. These applications help manufacturers maintain efficient operations.

Human resources applications support personnel management. Recruitment systems analyze candidate data to identify potential matches. Performance management tools track employee development. Resource planning systems optimize staffing levels. These applications help organizations manage their workforce effectively.

Marketing applications guide promotional efforts. Campaign analysis tools track performance and engagement. Customer segmentation systems identify target groups. Response prediction tools optimize timing and content. These applications help organizations implement effective marketing strategies.

Research applications support scientific investigation. Data analysis tools process experimental results. Pattern recognition systems identify relationships in complex datasets. Visualization tools communicate findings effectively. These applications help researchers understand complex phenomena.

Educational applications enhance learning processes. Student performance analysis identifies areas needing attention. Resource optimization tools manage educational materials. Administrative systems track operational requirements. These applications help educational institutions operate effectively.

Government applications serve various public needs. Policy analysis tools examine impact patterns. Resource management systems optimize service delivery. Public safety applications analyze incident patterns. These applications help government organizations serve constituents effectively.

Energy applications optimize resource usage. Consumption analysis predicts demand patterns. Distribution optimization reduces waste and improves efficiency. Maintenance planning prevents service interruptions. These applications help energy providers maintain reliable service.

Transportation applications enhance mobility services. Route optimization reduces travel time and fuel usage. Maintenance prediction prevents service interruptions. Resource management optimizes fleet utilization. These applications help transportation providers operate efficiently.

Agricultural applications optimize farming operations. Crop management systems analyze growing conditions. Resource optimization tools manage water and nutrient usage. Yield prediction helps planning and resource allocation. These applications help agricultural operations maintain productivity.

Construction applications support project management. Resource planning tools optimize material and labor usage. Progress tracking systems monitor project advancement. Cost management systems track expenses and variations. These applications help construction projects maintain efficiency.

Environmental applications monitor ecological factors. Pollution tracking systems analyze environmental impact. Resource management tools optimize conservation efforts. Climate analysis supports policy planning. These applications help organizations maintain environmental responsibility.

Security applications protect assets and operations. Threat detection systems analyze behavior patterns. Access management optimizes protection measures. Incident analysis supports response planning. These applications help organizations maintain operational security.

Technology applications support system operations. Performance analysis identifies optimization opportunities. Resource management tools optimize system usage. Development planning guides capability evolution. These applications help organizations maintain effective technology operations.

The practical impact of these applications continues to expand as technology advances and implementation experience grows. New capabilities emerge through ongoing development. Implementation options expand with growing experience. These developments create new opportunities for organizational improvement through data analysis.

The future of Data AI solutions continues to evolve through technological advancement and expanding implementation possibilities. Understanding emerging trends and potential developments helps organizations prepare for future capabilities while planning current implementations.

Automation capabilities continue to advance data processing efficiency. AutoML platforms expand their capabilities for model development and optimization. Automated data preparation tools improve efficiency while maintaining quality. Automated optimization systems enhance performance without manual intervention. These automation advances may reduce implementation complexity while improving operational efficiency.

Integration capabilities expand connection possibilities. New protocols enable more efficient data exchange between systems. Standards development improves interoperability across platforms. API evolution simplifies system connection. These integration advances may improve how organizations implement comprehensive solutions.

Edge computing is transforming data processing approaches. Local processing reduces central computing requirements while improving response times. Distributed analysis enables more efficient operation across locations. Edge-optimized models provide efficient local processing. These developments may change how organizations implement analytical capabilities.

Privacy-preserving techniques advance protection capabilities. Federated learning enables model training without centralizing sensitive data. Homomorphic encryption allows processing of encrypted data. Differential privacy protects individual information while maintaining analytical utility. These advances may enhance privacy protection while maintaining processing capabilities.

Quantum computing possibilities are emerging for specific applications. Quantum algorithms may enable more efficient processing of certain problems. Hybrid approaches might combine classical and quantum computing advantages. Early applications focus on optimization and simulation. These developments may create new analytical possibilities for specific use cases.

Real-time processing capabilities continue to advance. Stream processing enables immediate analysis of incoming data. Complex event processing identifies patterns in data flows. Immediate response systems enable rapid action on insights. These capabilities may enhance how organizations respond to changing conditions.

Model interpretability improves understanding of analytical processes. Explanation systems clarify how models reach conclusions. Visualization tools illustrate decision processes. Validation frameworks verify reasoning patterns. These advances may improve how organizations understand and trust analytical results.

Resource optimization continues to advance efficiency. New algorithms reduce computational requirements while maintaining accuracy. Hardware optimization improves processing efficiency. Implementation optimization enhances operational performance. These improvements may make sophisticated analysis more accessible across different scenarios.

Scalability options expand implementation possibilities. Cloud platforms provide flexible resource allocation. Distributed processing enables efficient operation across locations. Hybrid approaches combine different processing methods effectively. These advances may improve how organizations scale analytical capabilities.

Security measures continue to evolve with threats. New protection methods address emerging vulnerabilities. Enhanced monitoring improves threat detection. Automated response capabilities speed incident handling. These security advances may improve how organizations protect analytical operations.

Visualization capabilities are becoming more sophisticated. Interactive systems enable deeper data exploration. Virtual reality applications provide immersive data analysis.

Augmented reality enhances operational data visibility. These visualization advances may improve how organizations understand and communicate insights.

Natural language interfaces are improving system accessibility. Conversational interfaces enable natural interaction with analytical systems. Automated documentation enhances understanding of results. Natural query processing simplifies data exploration. These advances may improve how users interact with analytical capabilities.

Integration with artificial intelligence expands analytical possibilities. Machine learning enhances traditional statistical analysis. Deep learning enables processing of complex data types. Reinforcement learning optimizes operational decisions. These developments may create new analytical capabilities while improving existing approaches.

Regulatory frameworks continue to evolve around data analysis. Privacy regulations influence processing approaches. Industry standards guide implementation practices. International agreements affect cross-border operations. These regulatory developments may influence how organizations implement analytical capabilities.

Implementation practices continue to mature from experience. Best practices evolve for different scenarios. Standards develop for various applications. Quality frameworks guide implementation approaches. These developments may improve how organizations approach analytical implementation.

Cost structures evolve with technology advancement. New deployment options affect implementation expenses. Efficiency improvements influence operational costs. Resource optimization reduces processing expenses. These developments may change how organizations plan analytical implementations.

Support systems are becoming more sophisticated. Automated assistance improves issue resolution. Knowledge management enhances information access. Community

119

resources expand implementation guidance. These advances may improve how organizations maintain analytical capabilities.

Education and training approaches are evolving with requirements. New tools improve learning effectiveness. Online resources expand access to knowledge. Certification programs verify expertise levels. These developments may enhance how organizations build analytical capabilities.

The future suggests continuing evolution in analytical capabilities, implementation approaches, and operational practices. Organizations must maintain awareness of these developments while planning current implementations to ensure sustainable, effective solutions.

Our exploration of Data AI solutions has revealed the fundamental principles and practical applications that enable organizations to extract meaningful insights from their information resources. From examining core models and analytical tools to understanding implementation considerations and future developments, we've established a comprehensive foundation for effective data analysis implementation.

The principles we've explored regarding data processing, analysis, and interpretation apply similarly to other AI domains. Just as Data AI solutions transform raw information into actionable insights, other AI technologies process their specific types of input to generate valuable outputs. Understanding these parallel processing patterns helps organizations implement comprehensive AI strategies effectively.

As we move forward to examine Audio/Vision AI solutions, we'll explore how artificial intelligence processes and analyzes rich media content. Where Data AI solutions excel at structured information analysis, Audio/Vision AI enables sophisticated processing of sound and visual information. Many organizations implement both capabilities, using Data AI to analyze trends and patterns while leveraging

Audio/Vision AI to process images, video, and audio content.

The implementation considerations we've examined, from resource planning and security requirements to integration needs and operational management, remain relevant across AI domains. While specific technologies may differ, the fundamental principles of successful AI implementation persist. This understanding will prove valuable as we explore the unique characteristics and requirements of Audio/Vision AI solutions.

Our journey continues as we investigate how organizations leverage Audio/Vision AI to process and understand rich media content, enabling new possibilities in areas ranging from security and surveillance to entertainment and education. The exploration of these capabilities will further expand our understanding of AI's practical implementation possibilities.

GIL OREN

CHAPTER 6: AUDIO/VISION AI SOLUTIONS

Our exploration of artificial intelligence solutions now turns to the processing of rich media content through Audio/Vision AI. Where previous chapters examined the processing of language and data, we now investigate how AI systems understand and generate audio and visual information, enabling machines to interact with two fundamental aspects of human perception.

The evolution of Audio/Vision AI represents one of artificial intelligence's most visible achievements. From early experiments in pattern recognition to today's sophisticated systems capable of generating photorealistic images and understanding complex audio signals, these technologies have transformed how machines process sensory information. This progression enables applications ranging from security and surveillance to creative content generation.

The distinct yet related domains of audio and vision processing share common principles while maintaining unique characteristics. Audio processing systems analyze temporal patterns in sound waves, enabling speech recognition, music analysis, and sound generation. Vision systems examine spatial patterns in images and video, supporting object detection, scene understanding, and image creation. Understanding these parallel approaches helps organizations implement effective solutions.

The relationship between Audio/Vision AI and other AI domains proves particularly significant. While Language AI processes textual communication and Data AI analyzes both structured and unstructured information, Audio/Vision AI enables machines to understand and generate rich media content. Many applications combine these capabilities, creating comprehensive solutions that process multiple types of information simultaneously.

As we begin our examination of Audio/Vision AI solutions, we'll explore how organizations leverage these technologies to create practical applications. From understanding fundamental processing principles to examining specific implementation approaches, our journey reveals how these capabilities transform theoretical possibilities into practical solutions. The path ahead illuminates how Audio/Vision AI enables machines to perceive and interact with the world in increasingly sophisticated ways.

Audio/Vision AI solutions operate on fundamental principles of signal processing and pattern recognition. Understanding these foundations proves essential for effective implementation while revealing both the capabilities and limitations of current technologies.

Signal processing forms the basis of all audio/vision systems. Audio processing begins with the analysis of sound waves, converting acoustic energy into digital signals through sophisticated sampling techniques. Vision processing starts with the capture of light patterns, transforming optical information into digital representations through sensor arrays. These foundational processes enable all subsequent analysis and generation capabilities.

The digitization of audio signals involves specific technical considerations. Sampling rates determine temporal resolution, with higher rates capturing more detailed sound information. Bit depth affects amplitude precision, influencing the quality of sound reproduction. Understanding these parameters helps organizations implement appropriate audio processing solutions.

Visual information digitization presents parallel considerations. Spatial resolution determines the detail level in captured images. Color depth affects the range of reproducible colors. Frame rates influence temporal resolution in video capture. These fundamental characteristics shape vision processing capabilities.

Feature extraction represents a crucial step in both audio and vision processing. Audio systems identify characteristics like frequency components, temporal patterns, and amplitude variations. Vision systems detect edges, textures, colors, and spatial relationships. These extracted features enable higher-level understanding and analysis.

Pattern recognition builds upon feature extraction to enable sophisticated processing. Audio systems identify speech patterns, musical elements, or environmental sounds. Vision systems recognize objects, faces, text, or scene compositions. These recognition capabilities form the foundation for practical applications.

Quality management proves essential in audio/vision processing. Audio systems must maintain fidelity while managing noise and distortion. Vision systems need to handle varying lighting conditions and perspective changes. Understanding these quality factors helps guide effective implementation.

Neural network architectures play crucial roles in modern audio/vision systems. Convolutional networks excel at processing spatial patterns in images. Recurrent networks handle temporal patterns in audio signals. Understanding these architectural approaches helps explain both capabilities and requirements.

Training processes significantly influence system capabilities. Supervised learning uses labeled examples to teach pattern recognition. Unsupervised learning discovers patterns without explicit labeling. These training approaches shape how systems learn to process audio and visual information.

Resource requirements vary based on processing complexity. Real-time audio processing demands efficient computation for immediate response. High-resolution image processing requires substantial memory resources. Understanding these requirements helps organizations plan appropriate implementations.

Error handling represents a crucial consideration in audio/vision systems. Audio processing must manage background noise and signal interference. Vision systems need to handle occlusion and perspective variation. These error management capabilities help maintain reliable operation.

Performance optimization ensures efficient operation. Parallel processing enables faster computation of complex patterns. Hardware acceleration improves processing speed for specific operations. Understanding these optimization approaches helps create effective implementations.

Security considerations affect implementation approaches. Input validation prevents processing of malicious content. Output verification ensures appropriate generation results. These security measures help maintain safe operation.

Privacy management proves particularly important for audio/vision systems. Personal information often appears in images and audio recordings. Biometric data requires careful protection. Understanding these privacy implications helps guide appropriate implementation.

Standardization efforts influence implementation approaches. Audio formats define consistent ways to represent sound information. Image formats specify methods for encoding visual data. These standards help ensure compatibility across different systems.

Quality evaluation requires specific approaches for audio/vision processing. Audio quality metrics assess fidelity and clarity. Visual quality measures examine resolution and accuracy. These evaluation methods help maintain effective operation.

Integration capabilities significantly affect implementation success. Audio/vision systems must connect effectively with other components. Data exchange requires appropriate formats and protocols. Understanding these integration needs helps guide implementation planning.

Performance monitoring ensures reliable operation. Processing efficiency requires careful tracking. Resource utilization needs ongoing measurement. These monitoring capabilities help maintain effective solutions.

The evolution of audio/vision processing continues through technological advancement. New algorithms improve processing efficiency. Hardware developments enable enhanced capabilities. Understanding this evolution helps organizations plan sustainable implementations.

Future developments suggest continuing improvement in processing capabilities. Efficiency advances may reduce resource requirements. Quality improvements might enhance processing accuracy. These possibilities help guide implementation planning while maintaining current operational focus.

Audio AI models represent sophisticated approaches to sound processing and analysis. These models transform raw audio signals into meaningful information through various processing stages and analytical methods. Understanding these models and their capabilities proves essential for effective implementation.

Speech recognition models demonstrate significant advancement in audio processing. The wav2vec model, introduced by Facebook AI Research in 2019, revolutionized speech recognition through self-supervised learning approaches. This model learns speech representations from raw audio, enabling more accurate transcription across various languages and acoustic conditions.

OpenAI's Whisper, released in 2022, represents another significant advancement in speech recognition. Trained on 680,000 hours of multilingual and multitask supervised data, Whisper demonstrates robust performance across languages and domains. Its architecture combines transformer-based processing with sophisticated audio feature extraction.

Feature extraction forms a crucial foundation in audio processing. Models analyze characteristics like frequency components, temporal patterns, and amplitude variations. These extracted features enable higher-level understanding of audio content, from speech recognition to music analysis.

Voice processing models handle specific aspects of speech analysis. Speaker identification systems recognize individual voices through characteristic patterns. Emotion detection models analyze speech patterns for affective content. These specialized capabilities enable various practical applications.

Music processing models analyze musical content through sophisticated approaches. Pitch detection systems identify musical notes and harmonies. Rhythm analysis models examine temporal patterns in music. These capabilities support both analysis and generation of musical content.

Environmental sound recognition models process non-speech audio. These systems identify sounds from various sources, from machinery noise to natural environments. Such capabilities prove valuable for monitoring and security applications.

Sound quality analysis models evaluate audio characteristics. These systems assess factors like noise levels, distortion, and clarity. Such analysis helps maintain audio quality in various applications.

Generation models create synthetic audio content. Speech synthesis systems produce human-like voices. Music generation models create original compositions. These capabilities enable various creative and practical applications.

Training approaches significantly influence model capabilities. Supervised training uses labeled audio data for specific tasks. Self-supervised methods learn from unlabeled audio content. These training approaches shape how models process audio information.

Resource requirements vary between models. Some require substantial computing power for real-time processing. Others optimize for efficiency on limited resources. Understanding these requirements helps guide implementation planning.

Error handling capabilities ensure reliable operation. Models must manage background noise and interference. Recovery procedures address processing issues. These capabilities help maintain consistent performance.

Integration considerations affect implementation success. Models must connect effectively with other systems. Data exchange requires appropriate formats. Understanding these needs helps guide implementation planning.

Performance optimization ensures efficient operation. Models implement various techniques to improve processing speed. Resource management optimizes computational usage. These optimization approaches help maintain effective operation.

Security measures protect audio processing systems. Input validation prevents malicious content processing. Output verification ensures appropriate results. These measures help maintain safe operation.

Privacy protection proves particularly important for audio processing. Personal information in speech requires careful handling. Biometric voice data needs appropriate protection. These considerations help guide secure implementation.

Quality management ensures reliable processing. Models implement various techniques to maintain audio fidelity. Performance monitoring tracks processing accuracy. These practices help maintain effective operation.

Model selection significantly influences implementation success. Different models suit various processing needs.

Resource requirements affect deployment options. Understanding these factors helps guide appropriate selection.

Future developments suggest continuing advancement in audio processing. New architectures may improve processing efficiency. Training approaches might enhance accuracy. These possibilities help guide implementation planning.

The evolution of audio processing continues through technological advancement. New capabilities emerge from ongoing research. Implementation options expand with experience. Understanding this evolution helps organizations plan sustainable implementations.

Vision AI models represent sophisticated approaches to processing and understanding visual information. These models transform raw image and video data into meaningful insights through various processing stages and analytical methods. Understanding these models and their capabilities proves essential for effective implementation.

Stable Diffusion, released by Stability AI in 2022, represents a significant advancement in image generation capabilities. This open-source model demonstrates remarkable ability to create photorealistic images from text descriptions. Its architecture, based on latent diffusion models, enables efficient generation while maintaining high image quality.

The YOLO (You Only Look Once) framework, first introduced by Joseph Redmon in 2015 and continuously evolved through multiple versions, revolutionized real-time object detection. Its single-pass approach enables efficient processing of visual information, making it particularly valuable for applications requiring immediate response. Recent versions maintain this efficiency while improving accuracy.

Object detection models form a crucial component of vision processing. These systems identify and locate specific items within images or video streams. Different architectures balance speed and accuracy for various applications, from security monitoring to autonomous navigation.

Feature extraction represents a fundamental process in vision analysis. Models identify characteristics like edges, textures, colors, and spatial relationships. These extracted features enable higher-level understanding of visual content, supporting various recognition tasks.

Scene understanding models process overall image context. These systems analyze spatial relationships between objects, identify environmental characteristics, and interpret visual scenarios. Such capabilities enable comprehensive visual analysis.

Face recognition models implement specialized processing for human features. These systems identify facial characteristics, track expressions, and recognize individuals. Such capabilities require careful implementation to maintain both accuracy and appropriate use.

Quality analysis models evaluate image characteristics. These systems assess factors like resolution, clarity, and color accuracy. Such analysis helps maintain visual quality across different applications.

Generation models create synthetic visual content. Image synthesis systems produce original visuals from descriptions. Style transfer models modify existing images. These capabilities enable various creative and practical applications.

Training approaches significantly influence model capabilities. Supervised training uses labeled image data for specific tasks. Self-supervised methods learn from unlabeled visual content. These training approaches shape how models process visual information.

Resource requirements vary between models. Some demand substantial computing power for real-time processing. Others optimize for efficiency on limited resources. Understanding these requirements helps guide implementation planning.

Error handling capabilities ensure reliable operation. Models must manage varying lighting conditions and perspectives. Recovery procedures address processing issues.

These capabilities help maintain consistent performance.

Integration considerations affect implementation success. Models must connect effectively with other systems. Data exchange requires appropriate formats. Understanding these needs helps guide implementation planning.

Performance optimization ensures efficient operation. Models implement various techniques to improve processing speed. Resource management optimizes computational usage. These optimization approaches help maintain effective operation.

Security measures protect vision processing systems. Input validation prevents malicious content processing. Output verification ensures appropriate results. These measures help maintain safe operation.

Privacy protection proves particularly important for vision processing. Personal information in images requires careful handling. Biometric data needs appropriate protection. These considerations help guide secure implementation.

Quality management ensures reliable processing. Models implement various techniques to maintain image fidelity. Performance monitoring tracks processing accuracy. These practices help maintain effective operation.

Model selection significantly influences implementation success. Different models suit various processing needs. Resource requirements affect deployment options. Understanding these factors helps guide appropriate selection.

The relationship between different vision models shapes implementation approaches. Some applications combine multiple models for comprehensive processing. Others focus on specific capabilities for targeted needs. Understanding these relationships helps guide effective implementation.

Future developments suggest continuing advancement in vision processing. New architectures may improve processing efficiency. Training approaches might enhance accuracy. These possibilities help guide implementation planning while maintaining current operational focus.

The successful implementation of Audio/Vision AI solutions requires careful attention to numerous operational, technical, and organizational factors. Understanding these considerations helps ensure effective solution deployment while maintaining reliable operation.

Infrastructure planning forms a crucial foundation for implementation. Computing requirements vary significantly based on processing needs. Real-time video analysis demands substantial processing power, while basic audio processing might operate with more modest resources. Storage systems must handle large volumes of media data efficiently.

Network capabilities significantly influence implementation success. Bandwidth requirements vary based on data volume and processing approach. Real-time applications demand low-latency connections. Distributed processing requires reliable network infrastructure. Understanding these requirements helps plan appropriate network resources.

Data management proves particularly important for audio/vision implementations. Input data requires appropriate organization and storage. Processing results need efficient management systems. Archive requirements demand careful planning. These considerations help maintain effective data handling.

Security implementation demands comprehensive protection measures. Input validation prevents processing of malicious content. Access controls restrict system usage to authorized users. Encryption protects sensitive data during storage and transmission. These security measures help maintain appropriate protection.

Privacy management requires particular attention in audio/vision systems. Personal information appears frequently in images and audio. Biometric data demands careful protection. Regulatory requirements affect processing approaches. These privacy considerations guide appropriate implementation.

Performance optimization ensures reliable operation. Processing efficiency requires careful tuning. Resource utilization needs ongoing management. Scaling capabilities must match organizational requirements. Understanding these performance factors helps guide implementation planning.

Integration planning enables reliable system connection. APIs must support appropriate data exchange. Workflow integration maintains efficient operation. Error handling provides reliable recovery. These integration considerations help create effective solutions.

Quality management ensures reliable processing results. Input quality affects processing accuracy. Output quality requires careful verification. Performance monitoring tracks operational effectiveness. These quality measures help maintain reliable operation.

Resource planning extends beyond initial implementation. Ongoing operational needs require appropriate allocation. Growth requirements demand scalable resources. Maintenance needs ongoing support. Understanding these resource requirements helps guide effective planning.

Training requirements affect implementation success. Users need appropriate preparation for system operation. Administrators require operational knowledge. Support staff need troubleshooting expertise. These training needs help ensure effective system usage.

Documentation needs span multiple areas. Technical documentation supports implementation and maintenance. User documentation enables effective operation. Operational procedures guide ongoing management. These documentation requirements help maintain solution knowledge.

Testing requirements ensure reliable operation. Functional testing verifies basic capabilities. Performance testing confirms operational characteristics. Security testing validates protection measures. These testing considerations help maintain reliable solutions.

Monitoring capabilities support ongoing operation.

Performance monitoring tracks system behavior. Security monitoring identifies potential issues. Usage monitoring guides optimization efforts. These monitoring capabilities help maintain effective operation.

Disaster recovery planning ensures operational continuity. Backup procedures protect essential data and configurations. Recovery processes restore operation after issues. Testing validates recovery capabilities. These planning considerations help maintain reliable operation.

Version management maintains solution currency. Update procedures keep systems current. Testing processes verify changes. Rollback capabilities ensure reliability. These version management considerations help maintain effective solutions.

Cost management extends throughout implementation lifecycle. Infrastructure costs include computing and storage resources. Operational expenses cover maintenance and support. Growth costs require appropriate planning. These cost considerations help guide sustainable implementation.

Risk management addresses potential issues. Technical risks require appropriate mitigation. Operational risks need careful management. Strategic risks demand appropriate planning. These risk management considerations help maintain reliable operation.

Compliance requirements affect implementation approaches. Data protection regulations influence processing methods. Industry standards guide security measures. Documentation requirements ensure appropriate records. These compliance considerations help maintain regulatory alignment.

Future planning ensures sustainable implementation. Technology evolution requires ongoing attention. Capability needs continue to develop. Integration requirements evolve over time. These planning considerations help maintain effective solutions.

Audio/Vision tools transform theoretical capabilities into practical solutions, enabling organizations to implement sophisticated processing capabilities effectively. Understanding these tools, their capabilities, and implementation considerations proves essential for successful deployment.

DALL-E, introduced by OpenAI in 2021 and advanced with DALL-E 2 in 2022, represents significant progress in text-to-image generation tools. The system demonstrates sophisticated capabilities in creating detailed images from textual descriptions. This tool exemplifies how advanced models can be made accessible through practical interfaces.

Adobe Firefly, launched in 2023, integrates generative AI capabilities into professional creative workflows. The system provides various tools for image generation and manipulation while maintaining integration with existing Adobe products. Its development demonstrates how AI tools can enhance established creative processes.

OpenAI's Whisper implementation, made publicly available in 2022, provides practical tools for speech recognition and transcription. The system offers both command-line and API interfaces, enabling flexible implementation approaches. Its open-source nature allows organizations to adapt the tool for specific needs.

Development frameworks support implementation efforts. PyTorch provides comprehensive tools for both audio and vision processing. TensorFlow offers extensive capabilities for implementing various processing models. These frameworks enable effective solution development.

Integration tools enable connection with existing systems. API management tools handle communication between components. Data transformation tools prepare information for processing. Results management tools handle system outputs. These capabilities support effective integration.

Quality analysis tools ensure reliable processing. Audio analysis systems verify sound quality and clarity. Image analysis tools examine visual characteristics. Performance monitoring tracks processing effectiveness. These tools help maintain processing quality.

Testing tools support implementation validation. Functional testing verifies processing capabilities. Performance testing measures operational characteristics. Security testing confirms protection measures. These tools help ensure reliable operation.

Development environments support solution creation. Integrated development environments provide comprehensive tool access. Jupyter notebooks enable interactive development. Cloud platforms offer development and deployment capabilities. These environments help organizations create effective solutions.

Monitoring tools track operational performance. Usage monitoring measures system activity. Quality monitoring verifies processing accuracy. Security monitoring identifies potential issues. These capabilities help maintain effective operations.

Management tools support ongoing operation. Version control systems track solution changes. Configuration management maintains system settings. Resource management optimizes system operation. These tools help maintain effective solutions.

Security tools protect processing operations. Input validation prevents harmful content processing. Output filtering ensures appropriate results. Access control manages system usage. These capabilities help maintain secure operations.

Optimization tools improve solution performance. Caching systems speed response times. Load balancing distributes processing effectively. Resource management ensures efficient operation. These capabilities help maintain effective solutions.

Documentation tools support solution maintenance. API documentation describes integration capabilities. Operation guides explain system management. User guides support effective usage. These resources help maintain solution knowledge.

Training tools support user preparation. Tutorial systems explain solution capabilities. Practice environments enable safe learning. Reference materials provide ongoing support. These resources help prepare for effective solution usage.

Deployment tools enable solution implementation. Container systems provide consistent deployment. Orchestration tools manage system operation. Scaling tools handle growing requirements. These capabilities help implement effective solutions.

Analytics tools measure solution effectiveness. Usage analytics track system patterns. Performance analytics measure processing efficiency. Quality analytics verify output accuracy. These capabilities help evaluate and improve operations.

Support tools assist with ongoing operation. Problem tracking systems manage issue resolution. Knowledge bases provide solution information. Communication systems enable assistance access. These capabilities help maintain effective operations.

Visualization tools aid understanding of processing results. Audio visualization helps analyze sound patterns. Image visualization supports visual analysis. Performance visualization tracks operational metrics. These tools help understand system operation.

Integration frameworks support system connection. API frameworks enable systematic integration. Data exchange tools handle information transfer. Error management provides reliable recovery. These capabilities help create effective solutions.

The practical applications of Audio/Vision AI solutions demonstrate their transformative impact across various domains. Understanding these applications helps organizations identify implementation opportunities while providing concrete examples of successful deployment.

Creative content generation represents a significant application area. Professional design studios use image generation tools to accelerate concept development. Marketing teams leverage these capabilities for rapid content creation. Publishers implement audio processing for audiobook production. These applications demonstrate how Audio/Vision AI enhances creative workflows.

Security applications utilize sophisticated vision processing. Real-time monitoring systems employ object detection for surveillance. Access control systems implement face recognition for secure entry. Anomaly detection identifies unusual patterns in video streams. These implementations demonstrate practical security enhancement through AI.

Media production benefits from various Audio/Vision capabilities. Post-production teams use audio processing for sound enhancement. Video editors implement AI-powered effects and corrections. Quality control systems analyze content automatically. These applications streamline media production workflows.

Communications applications leverage both audio and vision processing. Video conferencing systems implement background modification and noise reduction. Translation systems provide real-time captioning. Recording systems enable automated transcription. These capabilities enhance remote communication effectiveness.

Entertainment applications demonstrate sophisticated implementation. Gaming systems use vision processing for player interaction. Virtual reality implements real-time environment generation. Augmented reality combines real and synthetic content. These applications create immersive user experiences.

Quality control applications ensure product consistency. Manufacturing systems inspect products visually. Audio analysis verifies equipment operation. Defect detection identifies production issues. These applications maintain production quality standards.

Documentation systems leverage multiple processing capabilities. Scanner systems implement text recognition from images. Audio recording enables voice documentation. Video analysis supports visual documentation. These applications enhance information capture and management.

Verification systems implement various authentication methods. Signature verification analyzes written marks. Voice authentication processes speech patterns. Face verification confirms identity through visual analysis. These applications enhance security while maintaining user convenience.

Transportation applications utilize vision processing extensively. Traffic monitoring systems analyze vehicle movement. Parking management implements vehicle detection. Safety systems monitor driver attention. These applications enhance transportation efficiency and safety.

Retail applications leverage various analytical capabilities. Store monitoring systems track customer movement. Inventory management implements product recognition. Security systems detect unusual behavior. These applications enhance retail operations.

Educational applications support learning processes. Distance learning systems implement student monitoring. Presentation tools enable automated captioning. Assessment systems analyze student performances. These applications enhance educational effectiveness.

Research applications support scientific investigation. Laboratory systems analyze experimental results. Data collection implements automated observation. Documentation systems record research activities. These applications enhance research efficiency.

Environmental monitoring implements various sensing capabilities. Wildlife tracking uses visual identification. Sound analysis monitors species populations. Change detection identifies environmental variations. These applications support environmental protection.

Construction applications enhance project management. Safety monitoring implements worker protection. Progress tracking analyzes site development. Quality control verifies construction standards. These applications improve construction efficiency.

Agricultural applications optimize farming operations. Crop monitoring implements growth analysis. Disease detection identifies plant issues. Yield assessment predicts harvest results. These applications enhance agricultural productivity.

Navigation systems utilize sophisticated vision processing. Mapping applications analyze environmental features. Guidance systems implement path planning. Obstacle detection ensures safe movement. These applications enable reliable navigation.

Performance analysis applications evaluate various activities. Sports analysis implements movement tracking. Performance monitoring analyzes execution patterns. Training systems provide automated feedback. These applications enhance performance improvement.

Documentation verification implements multiple analyses. Document authentication verifies authenticity. Content validation confirms accuracy. Version tracking maintains document history. These applications ensure documentation reliability.

Accessibility applications enhance information access. Text recognition enables document reading. Speech synthesis provides audio output. Visual assistance implements object identification. These applications support broader information access.

The future of Audio/Vision AI solutions continues to evolve through technological advancement and expanding implementation possibilities. Understanding emerging trends and potential developments helps organizations prepare for future capabilities while planning current implementations.

Processing efficiency continues to advance through various developments. New algorithms reduce computational requirements while maintaining accuracy. Hardware optimization improves processing speed and capacity.

141

Implementation approaches enhance operational efficiency. These advances may make sophisticated processing more accessible across different scenarios.

Model architectures continue to evolve with research progress. More efficient attention mechanisms may enable better performance with reduced resources. Advanced feature extraction approaches could improve processing accuracy. Novel neural network structures might enhance processing capabilities. These architectural developments may create new implementation possibilities.

Multimodal processing represents a significant development direction. The integration of audio, vision, and other modalities enables more comprehensive understanding. Combined processing approaches enhance analytical capabilities. Unified architectures support integrated processing. These capabilities suggest future applications combining multiple forms of perception.

Quality improvements continue through various advances. Enhanced resolution in visual processing enables more detailed analysis. Improved audio clarity supports better sound processing. More sophisticated noise reduction maintains signal quality. These quality advances may enhance processing accuracy and reliability.

Real-time processing capabilities continue to advance. Faster processing enables immediate response to audio/visual input. Enhanced streaming capabilities support continuous analysis. Improved latency management ensures timely processing. These capabilities may enhance interactive applications.

Edge processing continues to evolve for local implementation. Optimized models enable efficient local processing. Distributed architectures support coordinated analysis. Enhanced management systems maintain operational control. These developments may expand deployment possibilities.

Privacy-preserving techniques advance protection

capabilities. Local processing reduces data exposure risks. Encrypted computation enables secure processing. Anonymous analysis protects personal information. These developments may enhance privacy protection while maintaining processing capabilities.

Integration capabilities continue to expand through standardization. New protocols enable better system connection. Enhanced interfaces improve interoperability. Standardized formats support efficient data exchange. These advances may simplify how organizations implement Audio/Vision AI within existing operations.

Resource optimization continues to advance efficiency. New techniques reduce computational requirements. Enhanced memory management improves operation. Optimized storage approaches manage data effectively. These improvements may make sophisticated processing more widely accessible.

Security measures continue to evolve with threats. New protection methods address emerging vulnerabilities. Enhanced monitoring improves threat detection. Automated response capabilities speed incident handling. These security advances may improve how organizations protect Audio/Vision AI implementations.

Generation capabilities are becoming more sophisticated. Enhanced image synthesis produces more realistic results. Advanced audio generation creates more natural sound. Improved control enables precise output management. These capabilities may expand creative possibilities.

Quality evaluation continues to advance through new methods. Enhanced metrics provide better quality assessment. Automated analysis improves quality verification. Continuous monitoring ensures consistent operation. These advances may improve how organizations maintain processing quality.

Implementation practices continue to mature from experience. Best practices evolve for different scenarios. Standards develop for various applications. Quality frameworks guide implementation approaches. These developments may improve how organizations approach Audio/Vision AI implementation.

User interaction methods are becoming more sophisticated. Natural interfaces improve system accessibility. Multimodal interaction enables intuitive operation. Enhanced feedback provides better user guidance. These developments may enhance how users engage with Audio/Vision AI solutions.

Cost structures evolve with technology advancement. New deployment options affect implementation expenses. Efficiency improvements influence operational costs. Resource optimization reduces processing expenses. These developments may change how organizations plan Audio/Vision AI implementations.

Regulatory frameworks continue to evolve around Audio/Vision AI. Privacy regulations influence processing approaches. Security standards guide implementation practices. Compliance requirements affect operational procedures. These regulatory developments may influence how organizations implement and operate Audio/Vision AI solutions.

Support systems are becoming more sophisticated. Automated assistance improves issue resolution. Knowledge management enhances information access. Community resources expand implementation guidance. These advances may improve how organizations maintain Audio/Vision AI solutions.

The integration of artificial intelligence continues to advance processing capabilities. Machine learning enhances traditional processing approaches. Deep learning enables more sophisticated analysis. Reinforcement learning optimizes operational decisions. These developments may create new analytical capabilities while improving existing approaches.

The future suggests continuing evolution in processing capabilities, implementation approaches, and operational practices. Organizations must maintain awareness of these developments while planning current implementations to ensure sustainable, effective solutions.

Our exploration of Audio/Vision AI solutions has revealed the sophisticated capabilities that enable machines to process and understand rich media content. From examining fundamental processing principles to investigating practical applications, we've established a comprehensive foundation for implementing these transformative technologies.

The principles we've explored regarding audio and visual processing demonstrate how machines can interpret and analyze sensory information. These capabilities prove particularly relevant as we move forward to examine Healthcare AI solutions, where the processing of medical imaging, patient monitoring data, and diagnostic information combines multiple forms of analysis for critical healthcare applications.

The implementation considerations we've examined, from resource requirements and security measures to integration needs and operational management, remain relevant as we explore healthcare applications. While specific technologies may differ, the fundamental principles of successful AI implementation persist. This understanding will prove particularly valuable as we examine how healthcare organizations leverage AI capabilities for improved patient care.

The relationship between Audio/Vision AI and Healthcare AI illustrates the interconnected nature of AI domains. Medical imaging analysis requires sophisticated visual processing capabilities, while patient monitoring often involves both audio and visual data analysis. Understanding these relationships helps organizations implement comprehensive healthcare solutions that leverage multiple AI capabilities effectively.

Our journey continues as we examine how healthcare organizations implement AI solutions to enhance medical care, support clinical decisions, and improve patient outcomes. The exploration of Healthcare AI will reveal how organizations apply artificial intelligence to one of society's most crucial domains, while maintaining the careful balance between innovation and reliability that healthcare demands.

This transition from Audio/Vision AI to Healthcare AI represents more than a shift in application domain. It demonstrates how fundamental AI capabilities combine and evolve to address specific industry needs, creating solutions that transform theoretical possibilities into practical improvements in human well-being.

CHAPTER 7: HEALTHCARE AI SOLUTIONS

Our exploration of artificial intelligence solutions now turns to one of its most crucial applications: Healthcare AI. Where previous chapters examined the processing of language, data, and rich media content, we now investigate how AI systems enhance medical practice and improve patient care. This domain demonstrates how artificial intelligence directly impacts human well-being through sophisticated analysis and decision support.

The evolution of Healthcare AI represents a careful balance between technological innovation and clinical reliability. From early diagnostic support systems to today's sophisticated medical imaging analysis and clinical decision support tools, these technologies have transformed how healthcare providers diagnose conditions, plan treatments, and monitor patient outcomes. This progression demonstrates both the remarkable capabilities of AI and the rigorous requirements of medical applications.

The implementation of Healthcare AI involves unique considerations that distinguish it from other AI domains.

147

Medical applications demand exceptional accuracy, thorough validation, and careful attention to regulatory requirements. Patient privacy requires sophisticated protection, while clinical integration needs careful planning and validation. Understanding these requirements proves essential for successful implementation.

The relationship between Healthcare AI and previously examined domains proves particularly significant. Medical applications leverage language processing for clinical documentation, data analysis for patient records, and audio/vision processing for diagnostic imaging. This convergence of capabilities creates comprehensive solutions that support healthcare providers while improving patient care.

As we begin our examination of Healthcare AI solutions, we'll explore how organizations implement these technologies within strict medical requirements while maintaining practical effectiveness. From understanding fundamental principles to examining specific implementation approaches, our journey reveals how artificial intelligence enhances healthcare delivery while maintaining essential clinical standards. The path ahead illuminates how Healthcare AI transforms theoretical capabilities into practical improvements in medical care.

Healthcare AI solutions operate under unique principles that combine artificial intelligence capabilities with stringent medical requirements. Understanding these fundamentals proves essential for implementing solutions that meet both technological and clinical needs.

Medical data processing forms the foundation of Healthcare AI applications. Clinical data encompasses various types, from structured patient records and laboratory results to unstructured physician notes and diagnostic images. Each data type requires specific handling approaches while maintaining compliance with healthcare regulations such as HIPAA in the United States and GDPR in Europe.

Clinical decision support represents a crucial application of

148

Healthcare AI. These systems analyze patient data to assist healthcare providers in diagnosis and treatment planning. The development of such systems requires careful validation through clinical trials and peer review. Understanding these validation requirements helps guide appropriate implementation approaches.

Quality assurance in Healthcare AI demands rigorous attention. Systems must maintain consistent accuracy in medical analysis. Validation procedures verify processing reliability. Performance monitoring ensures ongoing effectiveness. These quality measures help maintain patient safety and clinical reliability.

Regulatory compliance significantly influences Healthcare AI implementation. The FDA's regulations for medical devices affect many Healthcare AI applications. European MDR requirements guide implementation in EU markets. International standards like ISO 13485 for medical devices shape development practices. Understanding these regulatory frameworks helps ensure compliant implementation.

Medical workflow integration requires careful consideration. Healthcare AI solutions must work effectively within existing clinical processes. Integration with Electronic Health Record (EHR) systems proves particularly crucial. Understanding these workflow requirements helps guide successful implementation.

Patient privacy protection demands sophisticated approaches. HIPAA requirements in the United States establish strict privacy standards. GDPR in Europe provides additional privacy frameworks. Various national regulations add further requirements. These privacy considerations significantly influence implementation approaches.

Clinical validation follows specific protocols in healthcare. Randomized controlled trials provide rigorous validation. Peer review ensures scientific validity. Ongoing monitoring tracks clinical effectiveness. These validation approaches help maintain medical reliability.

Performance requirements in healthcare applications exceed typical AI standards. Diagnostic accuracy must meet or exceed human capability. Response time needs careful optimization for clinical use. Reliability requirements demand consistent performance. Understanding these requirements helps guide appropriate implementation.

Risk management takes on particular importance in Healthcare AI. Patient safety requires careful consideration throughout development. Clinical risks need systematic management. Technical risks demand appropriate mitigation. These risk management practices help maintain safe operation.

Documentation requirements reflect healthcare standards. Clinical validation requires thorough documentation. Technical implementation needs detailed records. Operational procedures demand clear documentation. These requirements help maintain appropriate medical records.

Quality management systems ensure reliable operation. ISO 13485 provides framework guidance. FDA quality system regulations establish requirements. European MDR adds additional considerations. These quality systems help maintain reliable operation.

Implementation validation follows medical device standards. IEC 62304 guides software development. IEC 62366 addresses usability engineering. ISO 14971 guides risk management. These standards help ensure appropriate implementation.

Security requirements combine healthcare and technical needs. Patient data requires sophisticated protection. System access needs careful control. Operation monitoring ensures secure function. These security measures help maintain appropriate protection.

Clinical testing protocols ensure medical effectiveness. Validation studies verify clinical accuracy. User testing confirms practical utility. Performance testing ensures reliable operation. These testing approaches help maintain medical reliability.

Training requirements reflect healthcare needs. Clinical users need appropriate preparation. Technical staff require specific knowledge. Support personnel need operational understanding. These training needs help ensure effective system usage.

Integration planning addresses medical workflows. EHR integration enables efficient operation. Clinical process integration maintains effectiveness. Resource management optimizes operation. These integration considerations help create effective solutions.

Performance monitoring ensures ongoing effectiveness. Clinical accuracy requires continuous verification. Technical performance needs regular assessment. Operational efficiency demands ongoing monitoring. These monitoring practices help maintain reliable operation.

Future planning considers medical evolution. Clinical needs continue to develop. Technical capabilities advance regularly. Regulatory requirements evolve over time. These planning considerations help maintain effective solutions.

The evolution of Healthcare AI continues through careful advancement. New capabilities emerge through validated development. Implementation options expand with experience. These developments create new possibilities while maintaining medical reliability.

Medical imaging and analysis represent one of Healthcare AI's most significant applications. The integration of artificial intelligence with diagnostic imaging has transformed how healthcare providers examine and interpret medical images while maintaining clinical accuracy.

NVIDIA Clara, introduced in 2018 and continuously evolved, represents a comprehensive platform for medical imaging AI. The platform provides specialized tools for developing and deploying medical imaging applications, supporting various imaging modalities including X-ray, CT, MRI, and ultrasound. Its architecture enables efficient processing while maintaining medical accuracy requirements.

PathAI, founded in 2016, demonstrates specialized capabilities in pathology analysis. The system assists pathologists in analyzing tissue samples, particularly for cancer detection. Its implementation of machine learning techniques enhances diagnostic accuracy while maintaining compatibility with existing clinical workflows. This approach demonstrates how AI can augment rather than replace medical expertise.

Diagnostic imaging analysis follows specific medical protocols. Image preprocessing ensures consistent quality. Feature extraction identifies relevant medical indicators. Pattern recognition supports diagnostic assessment. These processes must maintain clinical accuracy while enabling efficient analysis.

Quality assurance in medical imaging requires rigorous attention. Image quality verification ensures reliable analysis. Processing validation confirms accurate interpretation. Result verification maintains diagnostic reliability. These quality measures help ensure clinical effectiveness.

Clinical validation for imaging systems follows strict protocols. Comparison studies verify accuracy against expert diagnosis. Performance analysis confirms reliable operation. Ongoing monitoring tracks clinical effectiveness. These validation approaches help maintain medical reliability.

Integration with clinical systems requires careful planning. PACS (Picture Archiving and Communication System) integration enables efficient workflow. EHR connection maintains comprehensive patient records. Reporting systems provide clear result communication. These integration capabilities help create effective solutions.

Performance optimization balances processing speed with accuracy. Real-time analysis supports immediate assessment when needed. Batch processing enables efficient handling of multiple cases. Resource management ensures reliable operation. These optimization approaches help maintain clinical effectiveness.

Security measures protect sensitive medical images. Access control restricts system usage to authorized personnel. Encryption protects data during storage and transmission. Audit trails track system usage. These security measures help maintain patient privacy.

Validation procedures ensure reliable operation. Clinical testing verifies diagnostic accuracy. Technical validation confirms processing reliability. User testing ensures practical effectiveness. These validation approaches help maintain medical standards.

Training requirements reflect clinical needs. Radiologists need understanding of AI capabilities and limitations. Technical staff require implementation knowledge. Support personnel need operational expertise. These training needs help ensure effective system usage.

Documentation requirements follow medical standards. Clinical validation requires thorough documentation. Technical implementation needs detailed records. Operational procedures demand clear guidelines. These documentation practices help maintain appropriate medical records.

Quality management ensures ongoing reliability. Performance monitoring tracks system accuracy. Resource utilization needs careful management. Error handling provides reliable recovery. These quality measures help maintain effective operation.

Risk management addresses clinical concerns. Patient safety requires careful consideration throughout development. Diagnostic reliability needs systematic verification. Technical risks demand appropriate mitigation. These risk management practices help maintain safe operation.

Regulatory compliance shapes implementation approaches. FDA requirements affect system development and deployment. European MDR guides implementation in EU markets. International standards influence development practices. These regulatory considerations help ensure compliant operation.

Implementation planning addresses clinical needs. Workflow integration maintains efficient operation. Resource allocation ensures reliable processing. Support systems enable effective maintenance. These planning considerations help create effective solutions.

Future developments suggest continuing advancement. New processing capabilities emerge through validated research. Implementation options expand with experience. These developments create new possibilities while maintaining medical reliability.

Clinical impact assessment guides development. Diagnostic accuracy improvements demonstrate value. Workflow efficiency gains support adoption. Cost-effectiveness analysis guides implementation. These assessments help validate implementation benefits.

Integration capabilities significantly affect implementation success. DICOM compliance enables standard image handling. HL7 support maintains healthcare system communication. API implementation enables system connection. These capabilities help create effective solutions.

The evolution of medical imaging AI continues through careful advancement. New capabilities emerge through validated development. Implementation options expand with experience. These developments create new possibilities while maintaining medical reliability.

Clinical data processing represents a fundamental component of Healthcare AI, transforming raw medical information into actionable clinical insights. This domain requires careful handling of sensitive patient information while maintaining medical accuracy and regulatory compliance.

Amazon Comprehend Medical, launched in 2018, exemplifies sophisticated medical text analysis capabilities. The service extracts relevant medical information from unstructured clinical notes, patient records, and medical literature. Its natural language processing capabilities maintain HIPAA compliance while enabling efficient information extraction from clinical documentation.

Clinical data types require specific handling approaches. Structured data includes laboratory results, vital signs, and medication records. Semi-structured data encompasses clinical notes and medical reports. Unstructured data contains imaging reports and consultation notes. Each type requires appropriate processing methods while maintaining medical accuracy.

Data quality management ensures reliable analysis. Validation procedures verify information accuracy. Standardization processes maintain consistent formats. Error detection identifies potential issues. These quality measures help ensure reliable clinical analysis.

Privacy protection implements sophisticated safeguards. De-identification removes personal information while maintaining clinical relevance. Encryption protects data during processing and storage. Access controls restrict information availability. These protection measures help maintain patient privacy.

Clinical terminology processing requires specialized approaches. Medical vocabulary systems like SNOMED CT and ICD-10 provide standardized terms. Natural language processing handles medical terminology variations. Concept mapping enables consistent understanding. These capabilities help maintain accurate clinical interpretation.

Integration with medical systems demands careful planning. EHR connection enables comprehensive patient information access. Laboratory system integration provides test result context. Pharmacy system connection maintains medication information. These integration capabilities help create complete clinical pictures.

Performance optimization ensures efficient operation. Processing speed meets clinical timing requirements. Resource utilization maintains system reliability. Error handling provides appropriate recovery. These optimization approaches help maintain effective operation.

Validation procedures verify processing accuracy. Clinical

accuracy testing confirms reliable interpretation. Technical validation verifies processing reliability. User testing ensures practical utility. These validation approaches help maintain medical standards.

Quality assurance implements rigorous controls. Data validation verifies information accuracy. Process monitoring ensures reliable operation. Result verification confirms analysis quality. These quality measures help maintain clinical reliability.

Documentation requirements follow medical standards. Processing procedures need clear documentation. Implementation details require thorough records. Operational guidelines demand clear presentation. These documentation practices help maintain appropriate medical records.

Security measures protect patient information. Access control restricts system usage. Encryption protects data confidentiality. Audit trails track information handling. These security measures help maintain patient privacy.

Clinical workflow integration ensures practical utility. Process integration maintains efficient operation. Information flow enables effective communication. Result delivery supports clinical decisions. These integration capabilities help create effective solutions.

Regulatory compliance guides implementation approaches. HIPAA requirements affect information handling. GDPR influences data protection measures. National regulations add specific requirements. These regulatory considerations help ensure compliant operation.

Training requirements reflect clinical needs. Medical staff need understanding of system capabilities. Technical personnel require implementation knowledge. Support staff need operational expertise. These training needs help ensure effective system usage.

Implementation planning addresses medical requirements. Workflow analysis guides system design. Resource planning ensures reliable operation. Support planning enables effective maintenance. These planning considerations help create effective solutions.

Performance monitoring ensures reliable operation. Accuracy tracking verifies processing reliability. Resource monitoring ensures efficient operation. Error detection enables quick response. These monitoring practices help maintain effective operation.

Future developments suggest continuing advancement. New processing capabilities emerge through validation. Implementation options expand with experience. These developments create new possibilities while maintaining medical reliability.

Impact assessment guides development decisions. Clinical utility demonstrates value. Workflow efficiency supports adoption. Cost-effectiveness guides implementation. These assessments help validate implementation benefits.

The evolution of clinical data processing continues through careful advancement. New capabilities emerge through validated development. Implementation options expand with experience. These developments create new possibilities while maintaining medical reliability.

The implementation of Healthcare AI solutions demands attention to unique considerations that combine medical requirements with technical capabilities. Understanding these considerations helps ensure successful deployment while maintaining clinical standards and regulatory compliance.

Infrastructure planning must address specific medical requirements. Computing systems need appropriate healthcare certification. Network infrastructure must maintain HIPAA compliance. Storage systems require secure medical data handling. These infrastructure considerations help create reliable clinical environments.

Clinical integration planning ensures practical utility. EHR integration maintains comprehensive patient records. Clinical workflow integration preserves operational efficiency. Department system integration enables complete information flow. Understanding these integration needs helps guide effective implementation.

Regulatory compliance shapes every implementation aspect. FDA requirements affect system classification and validation. HIPAA guidelines influence data handling and privacy protection. European MDR requirements guide EU market implementation. International standards like ISO 13485 and IEC 62304 establish development frameworks.

Privacy protection implements multiple security layers. Data encryption protects information during storage and transmission. Access control restricts system usage to authorized personnel. Audit trails track all system interactions. De-identification procedures protect patient privacy during analysis.

Performance requirements reflect clinical needs. Response time must meet medical workflow demands. Accuracy levels must achieve or exceed human capability. Reliability standards must ensure consistent operation. These performance considerations help maintain clinical effectiveness.

Quality assurance implements comprehensive validation. Clinical testing verifies medical accuracy. Technical validation confirms system reliability. User testing ensures practical utility. These validation approaches help maintain medical standards.

Risk management addresses multiple concern levels. Patient safety requires primary consideration. Clinical accuracy needs systematic verification. Technical reliability demands appropriate monitoring. These risk management practices help maintain safe operation.

Implementation validation follows medical device standards. IEC 62304 guides software development practices. IEC 62366 addresses usability engineering requirements. ISO 14971 establishes risk management frameworks. These standards help ensure appropriate implementation.

Documentation requirements span multiple areas. Clinical validation needs thorough documentation. Technical implementation requires detailed records. Operational procedures demand clear guidelines. These documentation practices help maintain appropriate medical records.

Training programs address various user needs. Clinical staff require understanding of system capabilities and limitations. Technical personnel need implementation knowledge. Support staff require operational expertise. These training considerations help ensure effective system usage.

Change management supports successful implementation. Process changes require careful planning and communication. User adoption needs appropriate support. Organization alignment ensures effective utilization. These change management practices help ensure implementation success.

Resource planning extends beyond initial implementation. Ongoing operational needs require appropriate allocation. Growth requirements demand scalable resources. Maintenance needs ongoing support. These resource considerations help maintain sustainable operation.

Testing requirements ensure reliable operation. Validation testing verifies clinical accuracy. Integration testing confirms system connections. Performance testing ensures reliable operation. These testing practices help maintain system reliability.

Monitoring capabilities support ongoing operation. Performance monitoring tracks system behavior. Security monitoring identifies potential issues. Usage monitoring guides optimization efforts. These monitoring practices help maintain effective operation.

Disaster recovery planning ensures operational continuity. Backup procedures protect essential data and configurations. Recovery processes restore operation after issues. Testing validates recovery capabilities. These planning considerations help maintain reliable operation.

Version management maintains solution currency. Update procedures keep systems current. Testing processes verify changes. Rollback capabilities ensure reliability. These version management practices help maintain effective solutions.

Support requirements ensure reliable operation. Technical support helps resolve issues. Clinical support assists with system usage. Development support aids implementation efforts. These support considerations help maintain effective solutions.

Quality management ensures reliable results. Validation procedures verify processing accuracy. Testing confirms operational reliability. Monitoring tracks ongoing performance. These quality considerations help maintain effective solutions.

Cost management extends beyond initial implementation. Infrastructure costs include computing and storage resources. Operational expenses cover maintenance and support. Growth costs require appropriate planning. These cost considerations help guide sustainable implementation.

Healthcare AI tools transform theoretical capabilities into practical medical solutions. These tools must meet stringent clinical requirements while enabling efficient implementation of AI capabilities in healthcare settings.

Google Health's platform, developed since 2006 and significantly advanced in recent years, represents a comprehensive approach to healthcare AI implementation. The platform provides tools for medical imaging analysis, clinical decision support, and healthcare data management. Its development reflects careful attention to medical requirements while maintaining technological sophistication.

Viz.ai, founded in 2016, demonstrates specialized capabilities in time-critical diagnosis. The platform's focus on stroke detection exemplifies how AI tools can address specific clinical needs. Its implementation of rapid notification systems and clinical workflow integration shows how AI tools can enhance urgent medical care while maintaining reliability.

Aidoc, established in 2016, showcases advanced medical imaging analysis tools. The system assists radiologists in detecting critical conditions through AI-powered analysis. Its always-on monitoring and prioritization capabilities demonstrate how AI tools can enhance clinical workflows while maintaining diagnostic accuracy.

Development tools support implementation efforts. Clinical validation tools verify medical accuracy. Integration frameworks enable system connection. Testing utilities ensure reliable operation. These development capabilities help create effective solutions.

Integration tools enable connection with medical systems. HL7 interfaces support healthcare system communication. DICOM tools enable medical image handling. API frameworks support system integration. These integration capabilities help create comprehensive solutions.

Validation tools ensure reliable operation. Clinical testing verifies medical accuracy. Technical validation confirms system reliability. User testing ensures practical utility. These validation capabilities help maintain medical standards.

Quality management tools support ongoing reliability. Performance monitoring tracks system accuracy. Resource utilization monitors system efficiency. Error tracking enables issue resolution. These quality tools help maintain effective operation.

Documentation tools support solution maintenance. Clinical documentation maintains medical records. Technical documentation describes system operation. User documentation enables effective usage. These documentation capabilities help maintain solution knowledge.

Training tools support user preparation. Tutorial systems explain solution capabilities. Practice environments enable safe learning. Reference materials provide ongoing support. These training capabilities help prepare for effective solution usage.

Deployment tools enable solution implementation. Container systems provide consistent deployment. Orchestration tools manage system operation. Scaling tools handle growing requirements. These deployment capabilities help implement effective solutions.

Analytics tools measure solution effectiveness. Usage analytics track system patterns. Performance analytics measure processing efficiency. Quality analytics verify output accuracy. These analytical capabilities help evaluate and improve operations.

Security tools protect medical operations. Access control manages system usage. Encryption protects sensitive data. Audit systems track system activity. These security capabilities help maintain patient privacy.

Monitoring tools track operational performance. Clinical accuracy monitoring verifies reliable operation. Resource monitoring ensures efficient usage. Security monitoring identifies potential issues. These monitoring capabilities help maintain effective operation.

Management tools support ongoing operation. Version control tracks system changes. Configuration management maintains settings. Resource management optimizes operation. These management capabilities help maintain effective solutions.

Support tools assist with issue resolution. Problem tracking manages issue handling. Knowledge bases provide solution information. Communication systems enable assistance access. These support capabilities help maintain reliable operation.

Testing tools verify solution reliability. Functional testing verifies basic operation. Performance testing confirms operational characteristics. Security testing validates protection measures. These testing capabilities help ensure reliable solutions.

Implementation tools support solution deployment. Workflow analysis guides implementation planning. Resource planning ensures appropriate allocation. Integration planning enables effective connection. These implementation capabilities help create effective solutions.

Optimization tools improve solution performance.

Processing optimization enhances efficiency. Resource optimization improves utilization. Integration optimization enhances system interaction. These optimization capabilities help maintain effective operation.

The evolution of healthcare tools continues through careful advancement. New capabilities emerge through validated development. Implementation options expand with experience. These developments create new possibilities while maintaining medical reliability.

The practical applications of Healthcare AI solutions demonstrate their transformative impact in medical settings. These implementations must maintain clinical accuracy and regulatory compliance while delivering tangible improvements in healthcare delivery.

Diagnostic support applications enhance clinical decision-making. Medical imaging analysis assists radiologists in identifying potential issues with increased accuracy and efficiency. Pathology systems support tissue sample analysis through pattern recognition. Laboratory result interpretation helps identify significant findings. These applications demonstrate how AI enhances diagnostic capabilities while maintaining medical accuracy.

Treatment planning systems support clinical decisions. Analysis of patient records helps identify appropriate treatment options. Clinical guideline integration ensures compliance with best practices. Outcome prediction assists in treatment selection. These applications help clinicians make informed decisions while maintaining medical standards.

Patient monitoring implements continuous analysis. Vital sign monitoring identifies potential issues early. Trend analysis tracks patient progress. Alert systems notify clinicians of significant changes. These applications enhance patient care while maintaining appropriate oversight.

Clinical research applications support medical advancement. Data analysis identifies patterns in large medical datasets. Trial matching helps connect patients with appropriate studies. Literature analysis supports research development. These applications accelerate medical research while maintaining scientific rigor.

Medical documentation applications enhance record keeping. Natural language processing extracts information from clinical notes. Automated coding assists with medical billing accuracy. Report generation supports clinical documentation. These applications improve efficiency while maintaining documentation standards.

Quality assurance applications monitor clinical performance. Process analysis identifies potential improvements. Outcome tracking measures treatment effectiveness. Compliance monitoring ensures regulatory adherence. These applications enhance healthcare quality while maintaining appropriate standards.

Resource management applications optimize healthcare delivery. Staff scheduling optimizes resource allocation. Equipment utilization tracking improves efficiency. Supply management ensures appropriate availability. These applications enhance operational efficiency while maintaining care quality.

Clinical training applications support medical education. Case simulation provides practical experience. Knowledge assessment tracks learning progress. Skill development supports clinical improvement. These applications enhance medical training while maintaining educational standards.

Workflow optimization applications improve operational efficiency. Process analysis identifies improvement opportunities. Task automation reduces manual effort. Integration optimization enhances system interaction. These applications improve efficiency while maintaining clinical accuracy.

Patient engagement applications enhance healthcare delivery. Communication systems support patient interaction. Education materials provide treatment information. Progress tracking encourages patient participation. These applications improve patient involvement while maintaining medical appropriateness.

Clinical communication applications enhance information sharing. Notification systems alert appropriate staff. Information sharing supports team coordination. Documentation sharing enables collaboration. These applications improve communication while maintaining privacy requirements.

Quality management applications ensure reliable care. Performance monitoring tracks clinical metrics. Process analysis identifies improvement needs. Compliance tracking ensures regulatory adherence. These applications maintain healthcare quality while supporting improvement.

Research support applications advance medical knowledge. Data analysis identifies research patterns. Literature review supports study development. Result validation ensures scientific reliability. These applications accelerate research while maintaining scientific standards.

Administrative applications support healthcare operations. Scheduling systems optimize resource usage. Billing systems ensure accurate charging. Compliance tracking maintains regulatory adherence. These applications improve operations while maintaining appropriate standards.

Emergency response applications support urgent care. Rapid diagnosis supports quick treatment decisions. Resource coordination enables effective response. Communication systems ensure information sharing. These applications enhance emergency care while maintaining medical standards.

Preventive care applications support health maintenance. Risk analysis identifies potential issues. Screening recommendations guide preventive care. Health monitoring tracks patient status. These applications enhance prevention while maintaining appropriate care standards.

Population health applications support broader healthcare management. Trend analysis identifies health patterns. Resource planning supports healthcare delivery. Outcome tracking measures intervention effectiveness. These applications improve population health while maintaining individual care standards.

Clinical decision support applications enhance medical practice. Evidence-based guidance supports treatment decisions. Risk assessment helps identify potential issues. Outcome prediction supports treatment planning. These applications improve clinical decisions while maintaining medical judgment.

The practical impact of these applications continues to expand through careful implementation. New capabilities emerge through validated development. Implementation options expand with experience. These developments create new possibilities while maintaining medical reliability.

The future of Healthcare AI solutions continues to evolve through careful advancement of both technological capabilities and clinical applications. Understanding emerging trends and potential developments helps organizations prepare for future capabilities while maintaining current medical standards.

Diagnostic accuracy continues to improve through various developments. Enhanced imaging analysis enables more precise detection of medical conditions. Advanced pattern recognition improves diagnostic reliability. Integration of multiple data sources supports comprehensive assessment. These advances may improve diagnostic capabilities while maintaining clinical standards.

Clinical decision support is advancing through sophisticated approaches. Evidence-based systems incorporate latest medical research. Personalized medicine approaches consider individual patient factors. Risk assessment improves through comprehensive data analysis. These developments may enhance clinical decision-making while maintaining medical judgment.

Patient monitoring capabilities are advancing through new technologies. Continuous analysis enables earlier detection of potential issues. Remote monitoring expands care possibilities. Integration of multiple data sources provides comprehensive assessment. These advances may improve patient care while maintaining appropriate oversight.

Privacy protection is advancing through new techniques. Enhanced encryption protects sensitive medical data. Improved access control maintains information security. Anonymous analysis enables research while protecting privacy. These developments may strengthen privacy protection while maintaining clinical utility.

Integration capabilities expand through standardization efforts. Enhanced interoperability enables better system connection. Improved data exchange supports comprehensive care. Standardized interfaces simplify implementation. These advances may improve system integration while maintaining security requirements.

Quality management is advancing through sophisticated approaches. Enhanced monitoring improves performance tracking. Advanced analytics identify improvement opportunities. Automated validation ensures reliable operation. These developments may improve quality assurance while maintaining efficiency.

Resource optimization continues through improved analysis. Enhanced scheduling optimizes resource allocation. Advanced planning improves resource utilization. Predictive analytics guide resource management. These advances may improve operational efficiency while maintaining care quality.

Clinical validation is advancing through refined methods. Enhanced testing approaches verify medical accuracy. Improved performance metrics track system reliability. Comprehensive validation ensures clinical effectiveness. These developments may improve validation while maintaining practical utility.

Training approaches are evolving to meet changing needs. Enhanced simulation provides realistic practice. Improved assessment tracks learning effectiveness. Personalized training adapts to individual needs. These advances may improve medical education while maintaining educational standards.

Security measures are advancing with emerging threats. Enhanced protection prevents unauthorized access. Improved monitoring identifies potential issues. Advanced response handles security incidents. These developments may strengthen security while maintaining operational efficiency.

Documentation systems are improving through enhanced capabilities. Automated recording maintains comprehensive records. Enhanced organization improves information access. Advanced search enables efficient retrieval. These advances may improve documentation while maintaining accuracy.

Research support is advancing through sophisticated analysis. Enhanced data processing identifies patterns. Improved validation ensures reliable results. Advanced collaboration supports research efforts. These developments may accelerate research while maintaining scientific rigor.

Implementation approaches are evolving through experience. Enhanced planning improves deployment success. Improved integration simplifies connection. Advanced management ensures reliable operation. These advances may improve implementation while maintaining medical standards.

Regulatory compliance is advancing through enhanced understanding. Improved frameworks guide implementation. Enhanced monitoring ensures adherence. Advanced documentation maintains compliance records. These developments may improve compliance while maintaining operational efficiency.

Cost management is improving through enhanced analysis. Better resource allocation optimizes expenses. Improved efficiency reduces operational costs. Advanced planning guides investment decisions. These advances may improve cost effectiveness while maintaining care quality.

Performance optimization continues through various approaches. Enhanced processing improves operational efficiency. Improved resource usage optimizes system operation. Advanced monitoring guides optimization efforts. These developments may improve performance while maintaining reliability.

Future possibilities are emerging through ongoing research. New capabilities advance through careful validation. Implementation options expand with experience. These developments create new opportunities while maintaining medical standards.

The integration of artificial intelligence in healthcare continues to advance through careful development. New capabilities emerge through validated research. Implementation options expand with growing experience. These developments may create new possibilities while maintaining essential medical standards.

The evolution suggests continuing advancement in capabilities, implementation approaches, and operational practices. Organizations must maintain awareness of these developments while planning current implementations to ensure sustainable, effective solutions that meet both current and future healthcare needs.

GIL OREN

CHAPTER 8: ROBOTICS AI SOLUTIONS

Our exploration of artificial intelligence solutions now enters the domain of physical interaction through Robotics AI. Where previous chapters examined the processing of information in various forms, we now investigate how AI systems control and coordinate physical movement while maintaining essential safety and reliability requirements.

The evolution of Robotics AI represents a crucial advancement in artificial intelligence applications. From early automated manufacturing systems to today's sophisticated robots capable of complex environmental interaction, these technologies have transformed how machines operate in the physical world. This progression demonstrates both the remarkable capabilities of AI and the critical importance of safety and reliability in physical systems.

The implementation of Robotics AI involves unique considerations that distinguish it from other AI domains. Physical interaction demands real-time processing and precise control while maintaining absolute safety. Environmental awareness requires sophisticated sensor integration and rapid

171

response capabilities. Understanding these requirements proves essential for successful implementation.

The relationship between Robotics AI and previously examined domains proves particularly significant. Robotic systems leverage language processing for interaction, data analysis for decision-making, and vision processing for environmental awareness. However, these capabilities must operate within strict real-time constraints while ensuring safe physical interaction. This convergence of capabilities creates comprehensive solutions that enable sophisticated robotic operations while maintaining essential safety standards.

As we begin our examination of Robotics AI solutions, we'll explore how organizations implement these technologies within strict safety requirements while maintaining practical effectiveness. From understanding fundamental principles of robotic control to examining specific implementation approaches, our journey reveals how artificial intelligence enables sophisticated physical interaction while maintaining essential operational standards. The path ahead illuminates how Robotics AI transforms theoretical capabilities into practical physical operations.

Robotics AI solutions operate under unique principles that combine artificial intelligence capabilities with physical control requirements. Understanding these fundamentals proves essential for implementing solutions that maintain both operational effectiveness and safety standards.

Real-time processing forms the foundation of Robotics AI applications. Unlike systems that process static information, robotic systems must continuously analyze sensor data and adjust physical actions within millisecond timeframes. This requirement shapes both hardware architecture and software design, demanding efficient processing while maintaining reliable operation.

Motion control represents a crucial capability in robotic systems. Precise movement requires sophisticated algorithms that account for physical dynamics, environmental conditions, and safety constraints. These control systems must maintain accuracy while adapting to changing conditions and potential disturbances.

Sensor integration enables environmental awareness. Multiple sensor types provide different data streams: cameras for visual information, LIDAR for distance measurement, touch sensors for physical contact detection. Integrating these inputs requires sophisticated processing while maintaining real-time response capabilities.

Safety systems implement multiple protection layers. Hardware safety circuits provide immediate response to dangerous conditions. Software safety systems monitor operation and prevent unsafe actions. Environmental monitoring ensures appropriate interaction with surroundings. These safety measures help maintain reliable protection.

Environmental interaction requires sophisticated processing. Object recognition identifies items in the robot's environment. Path planning determines safe movement routes. Collision avoidance prevents unwanted contact. These capabilities enable safe operation in dynamic environments.

Control architectures implement hierarchical processing. Low-level controllers manage immediate physical responses. Mid-level systems coordinate complex movements. High-level planning guides overall behavior. This hierarchical approach helps maintain reliable operation.

Performance monitoring ensures reliable operation. Position sensors track movement accuracy. Force sensors measure interaction pressures. Current monitoring detects motor loads. These monitoring systems help maintain safe operation.

Error handling implements multiple response levels. Immediate safety systems prevent dangerous conditions. Operational monitoring identifies potential issues. Recovery procedures address system problems. These error handling capabilities help maintain reliable operation.

Calibration systems ensure accurate operation. Sensor

calibration maintains input accuracy. Motor calibration ensures precise movement. System calibration coordinates multiple components. These calibration processes help maintain operational precision.

Integration capabilities enable system coordination. Component communication maintains synchronized operation. System coordination ensures efficient function. Error handling provides reliable recovery. These integration capabilities help create effective solutions.

Power management ensures reliable operation. Motor control optimizes power usage. System monitoring prevents overload conditions. Battery management maintains portable operation. These power management capabilities help maintain reliable function.

Thermal management prevents system problems. Component cooling maintains safe operation. Temperature monitoring prevents overheating. Thermal protection ensures system reliability. These thermal management capabilities help maintain reliable operation.

Mechanical integration requires careful consideration. Component mounting ensures stable operation. Cable management prevents interference. Maintenance access enables system service. These mechanical considerations help maintain reliable function.

Software architecture implements multiple layers. Real-time control manages immediate responses. Operational control coordinates system function. Strategic planning guides overall behavior. This layered approach helps maintain reliable operation.

Testing protocols verify system operation. Component testing verifies individual function. Integration testing confirms system coordination. Safety testing validates protection measures. These testing approaches help maintain reliable operation.

Documentation requirements reflect system complexity. Technical documentation describes system operation. Safety documentation specifies protection measures. Maintenance documentation guides system service. These documentation practices help maintain system knowledge.

Training requirements address multiple needs. Operator training ensures safe system use. Maintenance training enables system service. Development training supports system enhancement. These training needs help ensure effective system usage.

Implementation planning addresses operational needs. Infrastructure planning ensures appropriate support. Resource allocation maintains efficient operation. Integration planning enables effective coordination. These planning considerations help create effective solutions.

The evolution of Robotics AI continues through careful advancement. New capabilities emerge through validated development. Implementation options expand with experience. These developments create new possibilities while maintaining operational safety.

The development platforms supporting Robotics AI enable the creation and deployment of sophisticated robotic systems while maintaining essential safety and reliability requirements. Understanding these platforms proves crucial for effective implementation.

NVIDIA Isaac, introduced in 2018, represents a comprehensive platform for robotics development. The system combines simulation capabilities, AI training frameworks, and deployment tools within a unified environment. Its architecture enables development and testing of robotic systems while maintaining safety requirements through sophisticated simulation before physical deployment.

Simulation capabilities form a crucial component of development platforms. Virtual environments enable testing without physical risk. Physics engines provide realistic behavior modeling. Sensor simulation enables comprehensive testing. These simulation capabilities help ensure reliable development.

Training frameworks support AI development for robotics. Reinforcement learning enables behavior development through virtual practice. Supervised learning supports pattern recognition development. Transfer learning enables adaptation of existing capabilities. These training approaches help create effective solutions.

Control system development requires specific tools. Motion planning frameworks enable movement coordination. Path planning tools support navigation development. Object interaction systems enable manipulation control. These development capabilities help create reliable systems.

Safety validation implements multiple approaches. Virtual testing verifies basic operation. Simulation testing confirms safe behavior. Incremental deployment enables careful validation. These validation approaches help maintain safe operation.

Integration tools enable system development. Component libraries provide tested modules. Framework integration enables efficient development. Testing tools verify system operation. These integration capabilities help create effective solutions.

Performance optimization tools support development. Processing efficiency tools improve response time. Resource management optimizes system operation. Memory management ensures reliable function. These optimization capabilities help maintain effective operation.

Documentation systems support development efforts. API documentation describes interface capabilities. Implementation guides support system development. Example code demonstrates proper usage. These documentation resources help maintain development knowledge.

Version control manages development progress. Code management tracks system changes. Configuration control maintains system stability. Release management enables systematic deployment. These version control capabilities help maintain reliable development.

Testing frameworks verify system operation. Unit testing validates component function. Integration testing confirms system coordination. Performance testing verifies operational capabilities. These testing approaches help maintain reliable operation.

Deployment tools support system implementation. Configuration management maintains system settings. Resource allocation ensures efficient operation. Monitoring tools track system performance. These deployment capabilities help create effective solutions.

Debug tools support development efforts. Real-time monitoring tracks system operation. Error logging captures issue details. Analysis tools help identify problems. These debug capabilities help maintain development efficiency.

Community resources support development efforts. Knowledge sharing enables problem resolution. Component sharing accelerates development. Experience sharing guides implementation. These community resources help maintain development effectiveness.

Security tools protect system operation. Access control manages system usage. Encryption protects system communication. Monitoring tools track system activity. These security capabilities help maintain safe operation.

Performance analysis tools guide development. Processing efficiency measurement tracks system speed. Resource utilization monitoring ensures efficient operation. Quality metrics verify system reliability. These analysis capabilities help maintain effective development.

Hardware integration tools support physical systems. Sensor integration enables environmental awareness. Actuator control manages physical movement. Power management ensures reliable operation. These integration capabilities help create effective solutions.

Maintenance tools support ongoing operation. Diagnostic tools identify system issues. Calibration tools maintain system accuracy. Update tools manage system changes. These maintenance capabilities help maintain reliable operation.

Quality assurance tools verify system reliability. Testing frameworks confirm proper operation. Validation tools verify system safety. Monitoring tools track performance metrics. These quality tools help maintain reliable development.

The evolution of development platforms continues through careful advancement. New capabilities emerge through validated development. Implementation options expand with experience. These developments create new possibilities while maintaining development reliability.

Industrial robotics represents a fundamental application of Robotics AI, where artificial intelligence enhances manufacturing and production capabilities while maintaining strict safety and reliability requirements. Understanding these systems proves essential for effective implementation in industrial environments.

Manufacturing applications demonstrate sophisticated control requirements. Assembly operations demand precise movement coordination. Material handling requires careful object manipulation. Quality inspection needs accurate assessment capabilities. These applications showcase how AI enhances traditional robotics while maintaining industrial standards.

Safety systems implement multiple protection layers. Physical barriers prevent unauthorized access to operational areas. Light curtains detect potential intrusions. Emergency stop systems enable immediate shutdown. Monitoring systems track operational safety. These safety measures help maintain reliable protection in industrial settings.

Control systems maintain precise operation. Real-time controllers manage immediate movements. Programmable Logic Controllers (PLCs) coordinate system operations. Supervisory systems monitor overall function. These control systems help maintain reliable industrial operation.

Sensor integration enables environmental awareness.

178

Vision systems monitor work areas. Force sensors detect interaction pressures. Position sensors track movement accuracy. Proximity sensors prevent collisions. These sensor systems help maintain safe operation.

Quality control implements continuous monitoring. Vision inspection verifies product quality. Dimensional checking confirms specifications. Process monitoring ensures consistent operation. These quality measures help maintain production standards.

Maintenance systems ensure reliable operation. Predictive maintenance identifies potential issues. Preventive maintenance maintains system function. Corrective maintenance addresses problems quickly. These maintenance approaches help maintain operational reliability.

Integration capabilities connect multiple systems. Production planning systems coordinate operations. Inventory management tracks material flow. Quality systems monitor production results. These integration capabilities help create efficient operations.

Performance monitoring ensures efficient operation. Production rate tracking measures system speed. Quality metrics verify output consistency. Resource utilization monitors system efficiency. These monitoring capabilities help maintain effective operation.

Error handling implements multiple responses. Immediate safety systems prevent dangerous conditions. Production monitoring identifies quality issues. Recovery procedures address system problems. These error handling capabilities help maintain reliable operation.

Calibration systems maintain accuracy. Robot calibration ensures precise movement. Tool calibration maintains operational accuracy. System calibration coordinates multiple components. These calibration processes help maintain production quality.

Training systems support operational effectiveness. Operator training ensures safe system use. Maintenance

179

training enables system service. Programming training supports system configuration. These training capabilities help maintain effective operation.

Documentation systems maintain operational knowledge. Technical documentation describes system operation. Safety documentation specifies protection measures. Maintenance documentation guides system service. These documentation practices help maintain system knowledge.

Production planning tools support efficient operation. Schedule optimization maximizes system usage. Resource allocation ensures efficient operation. Material flow management maintains production continuity. These planning capabilities help create effective operations.

Quality assurance implements rigorous standards. Process monitoring ensures consistent operation. Product inspection verifies quality standards. System validation confirms reliable function. These quality measures help maintain production standards.

Safety validation implements multiple approaches. Risk assessment identifies potential hazards. Safety testing verifies protection measures. Operational monitoring ensures safe function. These validation approaches help maintain safe operation.

Efficiency optimization supports production goals. Process optimization improves operational speed. Resource optimization ensures efficient usage. Energy management reduces operational costs. These optimization capabilities help maintain efficient operation.

Integration planning ensures effective implementation. System coordination maintains synchronized operation. Resource management ensures efficient function. Error handling provides reliable recovery. These integration capabilities help create effective solutions.

Maintenance planning supports reliable operation. Preventive schedules maintain system function. Resource allocation ensures service capability. Documentation maintains service knowledge. These maintenance practices help maintain reliable operation.

The evolution of industrial robotics continues through careful advancement. New capabilities emerge through validated development. Implementation options expand with experience. These developments create new possibilities while maintaining operational safety.

The implementation of Robotics AI solutions demands attention to unique considerations that combine physical safety requirements with technical capabilities. Understanding these considerations helps ensure successful deployment while maintaining operational standards.

Physical infrastructure planning forms a crucial foundation. Floor space requirements must accommodate robot movement ranges. Power systems need appropriate capacity and reliability. Network infrastructure must support real-time communication. Environmental controls maintain appropriate operating conditions. These infrastructure considerations help create reliable operational environments.

Safety implementation demands comprehensive protection. Physical barriers prevent unauthorized access to operational areas. Sensor systems detect potential safety violations. Emergency stop systems enable immediate shutdown. Safety monitoring maintains continuous protection. These safety measures help maintain reliable operation.

Performance requirements reflect operational needs. Response time must meet real-time control demands. Accuracy levels must achieve production specifications. Reliability standards must ensure consistent operation. These performance considerations help maintain operational effectiveness.

Integration planning ensures practical utility. Production system integration maintains workflow efficiency. Control system integration enables coordinated operation. Monitoring system integration provides comprehensive oversight.

Understanding these integration needs helps guide effective implementation.

Maintenance requirements ensure ongoing reliability. Preventive maintenance schedules maintain system function. Spare parts management ensures repair capability. Technical support provides problem resolution. These maintenance considerations help maintain operational reliability.

Training programs address various user needs. Operator training ensures safe system operation. Maintenance training enables system service. Programming training supports system configuration. These training considerations help ensure effective system usage.

Risk management implements multiple approaches. Safety risk assessment identifies potential hazards. Operational risk evaluation guides implementation planning. Financial risk analysis supports investment decisions. These risk management practices help maintain safe operation.

Regulatory compliance shapes implementation approaches. Safety standards affect system design and operation. Industry regulations guide implementation requirements. Local codes influence installation specifications. These regulatory considerations help ensure compliant operation.

Documentation ' requirements span multiple areas. Technical documentation describes system operation. Safety documentation specifies protection measures. Maintenance documentation guides system service. These documentation practices help maintain appropriate records.

Testing protocols verify system operation. Component testing verifies individual function. Integration testing confirms system coordination. Safety testing validates protection measures. These testing practices help maintain system reliability.

Change management supports successful implementation. Process changes require careful planning and communication. User adoption needs appropriate support. Organization alignment ensures effective utilization. These change management practices help ensure implementation success.

Resource planning extends beyond initial implementation. Ongoing operational needs require appropriate allocation. Growth requirements demand scalable resources. Maintenance needs ongoing support. These resource considerations help maintain sustainable operation.

Quality assurance implements comprehensive validation. Operational testing verifies system function. Performance testing confirms operational characteristics. Safety testing validates protection measures. These quality measures help maintain system reliability.

Monitoring capabilities support ongoing operation. Performance monitoring tracks system behavior. Security monitoring identifies potential issues. Usage monitoring guides optimization efforts. These monitoring practices help maintain effective operation.

Disaster recovery planning ensures operational continuity. Backup procedures protect essential configurations. Recovery processes restore operation after issues. Testing validates recovery capabilities. These planning considerations help maintain reliable operation.

Version management maintains solution currency. Update procedures keep systems current. Testing processes verify changes. Rollback capabilities ensure reliability. These version management practices help maintain effective solutions.

Support requirements ensure reliable operation. Technical support helps resolve issues. Operational support assists with system usage. Development support aids implementation efforts. These support considerations help maintain effective solutions.

Cost management extends beyond initial implementation. Infrastructure costs include facility modifications and equipment. Operational expenses cover maintenance and support. Growth costs require appropriate planning. These cost considerations help guide sustainable implementation.

The evolution of implementation practices continues through careful advancement. New capabilities emerge through validated development. Implementation options expand with experience. These developments create new possibilities while maintaining operational safety.

Robotics AI tools transform theoretical capabilities into practical solutions, enabling organizations to implement sophisticated robotic systems while maintaining essential safety and operational requirements. Understanding these tools proves crucial for effective implementation.

Development frameworks support implementation efforts. Motion control libraries enable precise movement coordination. Sensor integration frameworks support environmental awareness. Communication tools enable system coordination. These development capabilities help create reliable solutions.

Control systems maintain operational reliability. Real-time controllers manage immediate responses. Motion planning tools coordinate complex movements. Path planning systems enable safe navigation. These control capabilities help maintain safe operation.

Safety tools implement protection measures. Safety monitoring tracks operational conditions. Emergency response systems handle critical situations. Access control manages system interaction. These safety capabilities help maintain reliable protection.

Integration platforms enable system coordination. Component communication maintains synchronized operation. System coordination ensures efficient function. Error handling provides reliable recovery. These integration capabilities help create effective solutions.

Monitoring tools track operational performance. Performance tracking measures system efficiency. Quality monitoring verifies operational accuracy. Resource monitoring ensures efficient usage. These monitoring capabilities help maintain effective operation.

Maintenance tools support system reliability. Diagnostic systems identify potential issues. Calibration tools maintain system accuracy. Update management ensures current operation. These maintenance capabilities help maintain reliable function.

Testing frameworks verify system operation. Functional testing confirms basic capabilities. Integration testing verifies system coordination. Safety testing validates protection measures. These testing capabilities help ensure reliable operation.

Documentation tools support solution maintenance. Technical documentation describes system operation. Safety documentation specifies protection measures. Maintenance documentation guides system service. These documentation capabilities help maintain system knowledge.

Simulation tools enable safe development. Virtual environments allow testing without physical risk. Physics engines provide realistic behavior modeling. Sensor simulation enables comprehensive testing. These simulation capabilities help ensure reliable development.

Programming tools support system configuration. Visual programming enables intuitive development. Text-based programming provides detailed control. Configuration tools manage system settings. These programming capabilities help create effective solutions.

Analysis tools measure system performance. Efficiency analysis tracks operational metrics. Quality analysis verifies system accuracy. Resource analysis ensures optimal usage. These analysis capabilities help maintain effective operation.

Validation tools verify system operation. Safety validation confirms protection measures. Performance validation verifies operational capability. Integration validation ensures reliable coordination. These validation capabilities help maintain reliable operation.

Optimization tools improve system performance. Motion optimization enhances operational efficiency. Resource

GIL OREN

optimization ensures efficient usage. Energy optimization reduces operational costs. These optimization capabilities help maintain efficient operation.

Configuration tools manage system settings. Parameter management maintains system control. Component configuration ensures proper operation. System coordination enables effective function. These configuration capabilities help create reliable solutions.

Deployment tools support system implementation. Installation tools enable proper setup. Configuration management maintains system settings. Monitoring tools track system performance. These deployment capabilities help create effective solutions.

Management tools support ongoing operation. Version control tracks system changes. Configuration control maintains stability. Resource management optimizes operation. These management capabilities help maintain reliable operation.

Security tools protect system function. Access control manages system usage. Communication security protects data exchange. Monitoring tools track system activity. These security capabilities help maintain safe operation.

Future developments continue to enhance tool capabilities. New functions emerge through validated development. Implementation options expand with experience. These developments create new possibilities while maintaining operational safety.

Integration tools enable comprehensive solutions. System connection maintains coordinated operation. Data exchange enables information flow. Error management provides reliable recovery. These integration capabilities help create effective solutions.

The practical applications of Robotics AI solutions demonstrate their transformative impact across various domains. Understanding these applications helps organizations identify implementation opportunities while

186

providing concrete examples of successful deployment.

Industrial automation represents a fundamental application area. Assembly operations implement precise component manipulation. Material handling systems manage inventory movement. Quality inspection systems verify product specifications. These applications demonstrate how Robotics AI enhances manufacturing efficiency while maintaining quality standards.

Maintenance operations benefit from robotic capabilities. Inspection systems examine equipment conditions in hazardous environments. Repair systems perform tasks in dangerous locations. Cleaning systems maintain facility conditions. These applications show how robotics enhances maintenance while improving safety.

Quality control applications leverage precise capabilities. Visual inspection systems verify product characteristics. Dimensional measurement confirms specifications. Surface analysis identifies defects. These applications demonstrate how robotics improves quality assurance while maintaining production speed.

Safety applications protect operational environments. Hazardous material handling reduces human exposure. Emergency response systems address dangerous situations. Environmental monitoring tracks safety conditions. These applications show how robotics enhances workplace safety.

Training systems support operational preparation. Simulation environments enable safe practice. Virtual reality provides immersive experience. Augmented reality guides operational procedures. These applications demonstrate how robotics enhances skill development.

Process optimization applications improve efficiency. Production flow analysis identifies improvement opportunities. Resource allocation optimizes system usage. Energy management reduces operational costs. These applications show how robotics enhances operational efficiency.

Integration applications connect multiple systems. Production coordination maintains workflow efficiency. Resource management ensures optimal usage. Quality tracking verifies operational results. These applications demonstrate how robotics enhances system coordination.

Validation applications verify system operation. Safety testing confirms protection measures. Performance testing verifies operational capability. Integration testing ensures reliable coordination. These applications show how robotics maintains operational reliability.

Documentation applications maintain system knowledge. Technical recording tracks system configuration. Operational logging maintains performance history. Maintenance tracking guides service requirements. These applications demonstrate how robotics supports system management.

Analysis applications measure operational effectiveness. Performance tracking verifies system efficiency. Quality monitoring ensures product consistency. Resource utilization optimizes system usage. These applications show how robotics enhances operational understanding.

Monitoring applications track system operation. Safety monitoring ensures protection measures. Performance tracking verifies operational efficiency. Quality monitoring maintains production standards. These applications demonstrate how robotics supports operational oversight.

Implementation applications support system deployment. Installation procedures guide system setup. Configuration management maintains settings. Testing verifies operational reliability. These applications show how robotics enables effective deployment.

Management applications support ongoing operation. Version control tracks system changes. Configuration control maintains stability. Resource management optimizes usage. These applications demonstrate how robotics supports operational management.

Security applications protect system operation. Access

control manages system usage. Communication security protects data exchange. Monitoring tracks system activity. These applications show how robotics maintains operational security.

Optimization applications improve system performance. Motion optimization enhances operational efficiency. Resource optimization ensures efficient usage. Energy optimization reduces costs. These applications demonstrate how robotics enhances operational efficiency.

Maintenance applications support system reliability. Diagnostic systems identify potential issues. Calibration maintains system accuracy. Update management ensures current operation. These applications show how robotics supports system reliability.

Integration applications enable comprehensive solutions. System connection maintains coordination. Data exchange enables information flow. Error management provides recovery. These applications demonstrate how robotics supports system integration.

Development applications support system creation. Programming tools enable system configuration. Testing verifies operational reliability. Documentation maintains system knowledge. These applications show how robotics supports system development.

Future applications continue to emerge through careful advancement. New capabilities emerge through validated development. Implementation options expand with experience. These developments create new possibilities while maintaining operational safety.

The future of Robotics AI solutions continues to evolve through careful advancement of both technological capabilities and practical applications. Understanding emerging trends and potential developments helps organizations prepare for future capabilities while maintaining operational standards.

Control system advancement promises enhanced

precision. Improved motion control enables more sophisticated movement. Enhanced sensor integration provides better environmental awareness. Advanced path planning enables more complex navigation. These developments may improve operational capabilities while maintaining safety requirements.

Safety systems continue to advance protection measures. Enhanced monitoring improves hazard detection. Advanced response systems handle emergencies more effectively. Improved coordination enables better protection. These developments may enhance safety while maintaining operational efficiency.

Integration capabilities expand through standardization efforts. Enhanced protocols enable better system connection. Improved data exchange supports comprehensive operation. Standardized interfaces simplify implementation. These advances may improve system integration while maintaining reliability.

Performance optimization continues through various approaches. Enhanced motion planning improves operational efficiency. Advanced resource management optimizes system usage. Improved energy management reduces operational costs. These developments may enhance efficiency while maintaining reliability.

Sensor technology advances are enabling better awareness. Enhanced vision systems improve environmental understanding. Advanced force sensing enables more precise interaction. Improved proximity detection prevents collisions more effectively. These developments may enhance operational awareness while maintaining safety.

Maintenance approaches are evolving through experience. Predictive capabilities identify potential issues earlier. Advanced diagnostics improve problem resolution. Enhanced calibration maintains system accuracy. These developments may improve reliability while reducing downtime.

Programming tools are becoming more sophisticated.

Enhanced visual programming improves accessibility. Advanced configuration tools enable better customization. Improved testing verifies operation more thoroughly. These developments may enhance implementation while maintaining reliability.

Simulation capabilities continue to advance. Enhanced physics modeling provides more realistic testing. Advanced sensor simulation enables better validation. Improved behavior modeling supports development. These developments may improve testing while reducing implementation risk.

Documentation systems are evolving to support complexity. Enhanced technical recording maintains system knowledge. Advanced operational logging tracks performance better. Improved maintenance tracking guides service more effectively. These developments may improve system management while maintaining reliability.

Analysis tools are advancing through new capabilities. Enhanced performance tracking provides better metrics. Advanced quality monitoring ensures consistent operation. Improved resource analysis optimizes usage more effectively. These developments may enhance operational understanding while maintaining efficiency.

Security measures are advancing with emerging threats. Enhanced access control protects system operation better. Advanced communication security improves data protection. Improved monitoring identifies issues more effectively. These developments may strengthen security while maintaining usability.

Training approaches are evolving to meet changing needs. Enhanced simulation provides more realistic practice. Advanced virtual reality improves immersion. Improved augmented reality guides operation better. These developments may enhance skill development while maintaining safety.

Implementation practices continue to mature. Enhanced

planning improves deployment success. Advanced integration simplifies connection. Improved management ensures reliable operation. These developments may improve implementation while maintaining standards.

Quality assurance is advancing through refined methods. Enhanced testing verifies operation more thoroughly. Advanced validation confirms reliability better. Improved monitoring tracks performance more effectively. These developments may improve quality while maintaining efficiency.

Cost management is improving through enhanced analysis. Better resource allocation optimizes expenses. Improved efficiency reduces operational costs. Advanced planning guides investment decisions. These developments may improve cost effectiveness while maintaining capability.

Regulatory compliance is advancing through enhanced understanding. Improved frameworks guide implementation better. Advanced monitoring ensures adherence more effectively. Enhanced documentation maintains compliance records better. These developments may improve compliance while maintaining operation.

Performance optimization continues through various approaches. Enhanced processing improves operational efficiency. Advanced resource usage optimizes system operation. Improved monitoring guides optimization efforts better. These developments may improve performance while maintaining reliability.

Future possibilities are emerging through ongoing research. New capabilities advance through careful validation. Implementation options expand with experience. These developments may create new opportunities while maintaining essential standards.

The evolution suggests continuing advancement in capabilities, implementation approaches, and operational practices. Organizations must maintain awareness of these developments while planning current implementations to ensure sustainable, effective solutions.

Our exploration of Robotics AI solutions has revealed how artificial intelligence enables sophisticated physical interaction while maintaining essential safety and operational standards. From examining fundamental principles of robotic control to investigating practical applications, we've established a comprehensive foundation for implementing these critical technologies within strict operational requirements.

The principles we've explored regarding safety systems, real-time control, and physical interaction demonstrate how AI implementations must adapt to the demands of operating in the physical world. These lessons prove particularly valuable as we move forward to examine Gaming AI solutions, where real-time interaction and complex decision-making take place within virtual environments that must maintain their own forms of reliability and performance standards.

The implementation considerations we've examined, from resource requirements and safety measures to integration needs and operational management, provide valuable context for understanding how organizations deploy sophisticated AI solutions. While specific technologies may differ, the fundamental principles of successful AI implementation persist. This understanding will prove particularly valuable as we examine how gaming organizations implement AI systems that must respond in real-time to player actions while maintaining consistent and engaging experiences.

The relationship between Robotics AI and Gaming AI illustrates important parallels in real-time operation and response requirements. Where robotic systems must ensure safe physical interaction through careful control and monitoring, gaming systems must ensure responsive and reliable virtual interaction through similar attention to performance and user experience. Understanding these parallels helps organizations implement comprehensive solutions that maintain appropriate standards in their respective domains.

Our journey continues as we examine how organizations implement Gaming AI solutions to enhance player experiences, create dynamic virtual environments, and enable sophisticated game mechanics. This transition from Robotics AI to Gaming AI represents more than a shift from physical to virtual domains, it demonstrates how artificial intelligence continues to expand its capabilities while maintaining essential requirements for reliable and engaging operation.

The path ahead reveals how organizations leverage AI capabilities in gaming systems, creating solutions that combine sophisticated decision-making with responsive interaction. This exploration will further expand our understanding of AI's practical implementation possibilities while maintaining focus on essential requirements for consistent and engaging operation.

CHAPTER 9: GAMING AI SOLUTIONS

Our exploration of artificial intelligence solutions now enters the dynamic realm of gaming, where AI systems must operate in real-time virtual environments while maintaining consistent and engaging user experiences. Where previous chapters examined AI's role in processing information and controlling physical systems, we now investigate how AI creates interactive experiences that respond intelligently to player actions.

The evolution of Gaming AI represents a significant advancement in artificial intelligence applications. From early rule-based game opponents to today's sophisticated systems capable of mastering complex strategies and generating dynamic content, these technologies have transformed how games operate and respond to players. This progression demonstrates both the remarkable capabilities of AI and the critical importance of maintaining engaging, responsive interaction in virtual environments.

The implementation of Gaming AI involves unique considerations that distinguish it from other AI domains. Real-time response demands immediate processing while maintaining consistent performance. Player interaction requires sophisticated decision-making that balances challenge with engagement. Environmental generation must create compelling spaces while maintaining performance requirements. Understanding these requirements proves essential for successful implementation.

The relationship between Gaming AI and previously examined domains proves particularly significant. Gaming systems leverage language processing for character interaction, data analysis for player behavior understanding, and vision processing for environmental awareness. However, these capabilities must operate within strict real-time constraints while ensuring consistent and engaging player experiences. This convergence of capabilities creates comprehensive solutions that enable sophisticated gaming experiences while maintaining essential performance standards.

As we begin our examination of Gaming AI solutions, we'll explore how organizations implement these technologies within strict performance requirements while maintaining player engagement. From understanding fundamental principles of game AI to examining specific implementation approaches, our journey reveals how artificial intelligence enables dynamic virtual experiences while maintaining essential operational standards. The path ahead illuminates how Gaming AI transforms theoretical capabilities into practical, engaging interactions within virtual worlds.

Gaming AI solutions operate under unique principles that combine artificial intelligence capabilities with real-time interactive requirements. Understanding these fundamentals proves essential for implementing solutions that maintain both performance standards and player engagement.

Real-time processing forms the foundation of Gaming AI applications. Unlike systems that can process information with flexible timing, gaming systems must respond to player actions immediately while maintaining consistent performance. This requirement shapes both system architecture and implementation approaches, demanding efficient processing while ensuring reliable operation.

Decision-making systems implement sophisticated logic. Game AI must evaluate situations, select appropriate responses, and execute actions within millisecond timeframes. These decisions must balance challenge and engagement, adapting to player skill levels while maintaining meaningful interaction. Understanding these decision-making requirements helps guide effective implementation.

Resource management ensures consistent performance. Memory usage must remain within defined limits while maintaining detailed environments. Processing power requires careful allocation across multiple AI systems. Network resources need efficient utilization for multiplayer experiences. These resource considerations help maintain reliable operation.

State management tracks game conditions. Environmental states record world conditions. Player states maintain interaction history. AI states track decision-making context. These state management systems help maintain consistent operation while enabling meaningful interaction.

Performance monitoring ensures reliable operation. Frame rate tracking verifies smooth visualization. Response time measurement confirms immediate interaction. Resource utilization monitors system efficiency. These monitoring systems help maintain consistent player experience.

Error handling implements multiple response levels. Input validation ensures appropriate player interaction. State verification maintains consistent operation. Recovery procedures address system issues. These error handling capabilities help maintain reliable operation.

Quality assurance implements specific approaches. Performance testing verifies consistent operation. Interaction testing confirms appropriate responses. Balance testing ensures engaging gameplay. These quality measures help maintain player engagement.

Player experience management guides implementation. Difficulty adaptation maintains appropriate challenge. Reward systems encourage continued engagement. Progress tracking enables meaningful advancement. These management systems help create engaging experiences.

Environmental awareness enables meaningful interaction. Spatial understanding guides AI movement. Object interaction maintains realistic behavior. Event response enables appropriate reactions. These awareness capabilities help create believable virtual worlds.

Interaction models guide AI behavior. Character personalities maintain consistent responses. Behavioral patterns create recognizable actions. Learning systems enable adaptation to player strategies. These interaction models help create engaging experiences.

Performance optimization ensures consistent operation. Processing efficiency maintains immediate response. Memory management ensures reliable function. Resource allocation optimizes system usage. These optimization approaches help maintain reliable operation.

Testing protocols verify system operation. Functional testing confirms basic capabilities. Integration testing verifies system coordination. Performance testing validates operational reliability. These testing approaches help maintain consistent operation.

Documentation requirements reflect system complexity. Technical documentation describes system operation. Integration documentation guides system connection. Maintenance documentation supports ongoing operation. These documentation practices help maintain system knowledge.

Integration capabilities enable system coordination. Component communication maintains synchronized operation. System coordination ensures efficient function. Error handling provides reliable recovery. These integration capabilities help create effective solutions.

Security measures protect system operation. Input validation prevents exploitation. State verification maintains fair play. Monitoring systems track unusual behavior. These security measures help maintain reliable operation.

Quality management ensures consistent experience. Performance monitoring tracks system behavior. Player feedback guides improvements. Analytics measure engagement levels. These quality measures help maintain effective operation.

Implementation planning addresses operational needs. Resource allocation ensures appropriate support. Integration planning enables effective coordination. Performance management maintains reliable operation. These planning considerations help create effective solutions.

The evolution of Gaming AI continues through careful advancement. New capabilities emerge through validated development. Implementation options expand with experience. These developments create new possibilities while maintaining operational reliability.

Core Gaming AI models represent sophisticated approaches to creating intelligent, responsive game experiences. Understanding these models and their capabilities proves essential for effective implementation in gaming environments.

AlphaStar, developed by DeepMind and unveiled in 2019, demonstrates advanced capabilities in strategic decision-making. The system masters complex real-time strategy games through sophisticated neural network architectures and reinforcement learning approaches. Its ability to manage resources, develop strategies, and adapt to opponent actions showcases how AI can handle complex game scenarios while maintaining competitive gameplay.

NVIDIA GameGAN, introduced in 2020, represents significant advancement in game environment generation. This generative adversarial network learns to create game environments by observing gameplay sequences. The system demonstrates how AI can generate interactive spaces that maintain both visual quality and functional gameplay mechanics while operating within performance constraints.

Decision-making models implement sophisticated strategies. Reinforcement learning enables adaptation to player behavior. Pattern recognition identifies effective tactics. Strategic planning balances immediate actions with long-term goals. These capabilities help create engaging AI opponents.

Environmental generation models create dynamic spaces. Procedural generation creates varied landscapes. Rule-based systems ensure playable spaces. Quality verification maintains consistent standards. These generation capabilities help create diverse game worlds.

Character behavior models enable believable interaction. Personality systems maintain consistent responses. Learning mechanisms adapt to player patterns. Social modeling enables group behavior. These behavioral capabilities help create engaging non-player characters.

Physics simulation models maintain realistic interaction. Movement systems calculate appropriate motion. Collision detection prevents unrealistic behavior. Environmental interaction maintains consistent response. These simulation capabilities help create believable environments.

Path-finding models enable intelligent movement. Navigation meshes guide valid paths. Obstacle avoidance prevents unrealistic motion. Goal planning enables purposeful movement. These movement capabilities help create realistic character behavior.

Resource management models optimize game operation. Memory allocation maintains efficient usage. Processing distribution ensures balanced load. Network utilization optimizes multiplayer interaction. These management capabilities help maintain consistent performance.

Combat systems implement balanced interaction. Tactical decision-making enables strategic combat. Skill system modeling maintains appropriate challenge. Damage calculation ensures fair interaction. These combat capabilities help create engaging conflicts.

Quest generation models create meaningful objectives. Story generation maintains narrative consistency. Goal creation ensures engaging tasks. Reward balancing maintains player motivation. These generation capabilities help create compelling gameplay.

Learning models enable AI adaptation. Strategy refinement improves decision-making. Pattern recognition identifies effective approaches. Performance optimization enhances operation. These learning capabilities help create evolving gameplay.

Testing models verify system operation. Performance validation ensures consistent operation. Balance testing confirms fair gameplay. Integration testing verifies system coordination. These testing capabilities help maintain reliable operation.

Optimization models improve system performance. Resource usage maintains efficient operation. Response time ensures immediate interaction. Quality management maintains consistent experience. These optimization capabilities help create reliable solutions.

Security models protect game integrity. Input validation prevents exploitation. State verification maintains fair play. Monitoring identifies unusual behavior. These security capabilities help maintain reliable operation.

Integration models enable system coordination. Component communication maintains synchronized operation. System coordination ensures efficient function. Error handling provides reliable recovery. These integration capabilities help create effective solutions.

Documentation models maintain system knowledge. Technical recording describes system operation. Integration guidance supports system connection. Maintenance information guides ongoing operation. These documentation

GIL OREN

capabilities help maintain system understanding.

Training models support system preparation. Initial learning establishes basic capabilities. Ongoing adaptation improves performance. Experience refinement enhances operation. These training capabilities help create effective systems.

Quality assurance models verify system operation. Performance testing confirms reliable operation. Integration testing verifies system coordination. Balance testing ensures fair gameplay. These quality capabilities help maintain effective operation.

The evolution of gaming models continues through careful advancement. New capabilities emerge through validated development. Implementation options expand with experience. These developments create new possibilities while maintaining operational reliability.

Game development platforms provide the foundational environments where Gaming AI solutions are created, tested, and implemented. Understanding these platforms proves essential for effective development and deployment of AI-enhanced gaming experiences.

Development environments support AI implementation. Integrated development environments provide comprehensive tool access. Testing frameworks enable systematic validation. Deployment tools support efficient distribution. These development capabilities help create effective solutions.

Asset generation systems enable content creation. Leonardo AI, introduced in 2022, provides sophisticated tools for creating game assets through AI-driven generation. The platform enables rapid development of visual content while maintaining quality standards and performance requirements.

Character creation platforms support AI-driven personalities. InWorld's platform, launched in 2021, enables the development of interactive non-player characters through sophisticated AI models. The system demonstrates how platforms can combine multiple AI capabilities to create engaging character interactions.

Environment building tools support world creation. Procedural generation platforms enable diverse landscape creation. Architecture systems maintain structural consistency. Population tools create believable spaces. These environmental capabilities help create immersive game worlds.

Testing frameworks verify system operation. Performance testing ensures consistent operation. Integration testing confirms system coordination. Balance testing validates gameplay fairness. These testing capabilities help maintain reliable operation.

Resource management platforms optimize system usage. Memory allocation tools ensure efficient operation. Processing distribution maintains balanced load. Network optimization supports multiplayer interaction. These management capabilities help create efficient solutions.

Quality assurance platforms maintain development standards. Automated testing verifies system operation. Performance monitoring tracks system behavior. Bug tracking manages issue resolution. These quality capabilities help maintain reliable development.

Integration platforms enable system coordination. Component connection maintains synchronized operation. System coordination ensures efficient function. Error handling provides reliable recovery. These integration capabilities help create effective solutions.

Documentation platforms support development knowledge. Technical documentation describes system operation. Integration documentation guides system connection. Maintenance documentation supports ongoing operation. These documentation capabilities help maintain system understanding.

Version control platforms manage development progress. Code management tracks system changes. Asset versioning maintains content organization. Release management enables systematic deployment. These version control capabilities help maintain reliable development.

Deployment platforms support system distribution. Build management creates release versions. Distribution tools enable efficient delivery. Update management maintains current versions. These deployment capabilities help maintain effective distribution.

Debug platforms support development efforts. Real-time monitoring tracks system operation. Error logging captures issue details. Analysis tools help identify problems. These debug capabilities help maintain development efficiency.

Community platforms support development efforts. Knowledge sharing enables problem resolution. Asset sharing accelerates development. Experience sharing guides implementation. These community capabilities help maintain development effectiveness.

Security platforms protect development assets. Access control manages system usage. Encryption protects sensitive content. Monitoring tools track system activity. These security capabilities help maintain safe operation.

Performance analysis platforms guide development. Processing efficiency measurement tracks system speed. Resource utilization monitoring ensures efficient operation. Quality metrics verify system reliability. These analysis capabilities help maintain effective development.

Training platforms support developer preparation. Tutorial systems explain platform capabilities. Practice environments enable safe learning. Reference materials provide ongoing support. These training capabilities help prepare for effective platform usage.

Maintenance platforms support ongoing operation. Update tools manage system changes. Diagnostic tools identify system issues. Recovery tools address operational problems. These maintenance capabilities help maintain reliable operation.

The evolution of development platforms continues

through careful advancement. New capabilities emerge through validated development. Implementation options expand with experience. These developments create new possibilities while maintaining development reliability.

The implementation of Gaming AI solutions demands attention to unique considerations that combine performance requirements with player engagement needs. Understanding these considerations helps ensure successful deployment while maintaining both technical standards and gaming experience.

Performance requirements form a crucial foundation. Frame rate consistency must maintain smooth visualization. Response time needs immediate interaction capability. Resource usage requires efficient operation. These performance considerations help create reliable gaming experiences.

Player experience management shapes implementation approaches. Difficulty balancing maintains appropriate challenge levels. Reward systems encourage continued engagement. Progress tracking enables meaningful advancement. Learning curves support skill development. These management considerations help create engaging experiences.

Resource planning addresses multiple needs. Computing requirements must support real-time operation. Memory management needs efficient organization. Storage systems require appropriate capacity. Network infrastructure must support multiplayer interaction. These resource considerations help maintain reliable operation.

Quality assurance implements comprehensive validation. Performance testing verifies system reliability. Gameplay testing confirms engaging interaction. Balance testing ensures fair challenge. Integration testing validates system coordination. These quality measures help maintain effective operation.

Integration planning ensures practical implementation. Game engine integration maintains efficient operation. Asset management enables effective content delivery. AI system coordination ensures synchronized behavior. Network systems support multiplayer functions. These integration considerations help create effective solutions.

Testing protocols verify system operation. Unit testing validates component function. Integration testing confirms system coordination. Performance testing ensures reliable operation. User testing validates player experience. These testing approaches help maintain reliable systems.

Security implementation protects gaming integrity. Input validation prevents exploitation. State verification maintains fair play. Anti-cheat systems protect competitive balance. Monitoring identifies unusual behavior. These security measures help maintain reliable operation.

Documentation requirements span multiple areas. Technical documentation describes system operation. Integration documentation guides system connection. Maintenance documentation supports ongoing operation. User documentation enables effective gameplay. These documentation practices help maintain system knowledge.

Performance optimization ensures reliable operation. Code optimization improves processing efficiency. Memory management maintains efficient resource usage. Network optimization reduces latency impact. These optimization approaches help maintain consistent operation.

Error handling implements multiple responses. Input validation ensures appropriate interaction. State verification maintains consistent operation. Recovery procedures address system issues. These error handling capabilities help maintain reliable operation.

Version management maintains system currency. Update procedures keep systems current. Testing processes verify changes. Rollback capabilities ensure reliability. Distribution systems enable efficient delivery. These version management practices help maintain effective solutions.

Asset management supports content delivery. Model

management maintains AI components. Visual asset organization enables efficient access. Audio content management supports immersive experience. These management practices help maintain effective operation.

Community management supports ongoing operation. Player feedback guides improvements. Issue tracking manages problem resolution. Update communication maintains user awareness. These management practices help maintain effective engagement.

Training requirements address multiple needs. Developer training ensures effective implementation. Player tutorials enable effective gameplay. Support training maintains operational assistance. These training considerations help ensure effective system usage.

Monitoring capabilities support ongoing operation. Performance monitoring tracks system behavior. Player behavior analysis guides improvements. Resource utilization ensures efficient operation. These monitoring practices help maintain effective solutions.

Cost management extends beyond initial implementation. Development costs include system creation. Operational expenses cover ongoing maintenance. Growth costs require appropriate planning. These cost considerations help guide sustainable implementation.

Scalability planning ensures growth capability. Player capacity planning supports expansion. Resource scaling enables increased usage. Performance maintenance ensures consistent operation. These scaling considerations help maintain reliable growth.

Quality management ensures consistent experience. Performance standards maintain reliable operation. Player experience metrics track engagement. System reliability measures verify operation. These quality considerations help maintain effective solutions.

The evolution of implementation practices continues through careful advancement. New capabilities emerge through validated development. Implementation options expand with experience. These developments create new possibilities while maintaining operational reliability.

Gaming AI tools transform theoretical capabilities into practical gaming solutions, enabling developers to implement sophisticated AI systems while maintaining performance requirements and player engagement. Understanding these tools proves crucial for effective implementation.

Development frameworks support implementation efforts. Game AI libraries enable sophisticated behavior creation. Physics engines maintain realistic interaction. Graphics frameworks support visual presentation. Animation systems enable fluid movement. These development capabilities help create engaging solutions.

Asset generation tools enable content creation. Environmental generators create diverse game worlds. Character creators develop varied personalities. Texture generators produce detailed surfaces. Sound generators create atmospheric audio. These generation capabilities help maintain rich content while reducing development time.

Testing tools verify system operation. Performance testing ensures consistent frame rates. AI behavior testing confirms appropriate responses. Integration testing verifies system coordination. Player experience testing validates engagement. These testing capabilities help maintain reliable operation.

Debug tools support development efforts. Real-time monitoring tracks system behavior. Error logging captures issue details. Performance profiling identifies bottlenecks. State inspection examines system conditions. These debug capabilities help maintain development efficiency.

Integration tools enable system coordination. Component communication maintains synchronized operation. Asset management ensures efficient access. Resource coordination optimizes system usage. Error handling provides reliable recovery. These integration capabilities help create effective solutions.

Monitoring tools track operational performance. Frame rate monitoring ensures smooth visualization. Resource utilization tracks system efficiency. Player behavior analysis guides improvements. Network performance ensures reliable multiplayer. These monitoring capabilities help maintain effective operation.

Performance tools optimize system operation. Code optimization improves processing efficiency. Memory management ensures efficient resource usage. Network optimization reduces latency impact. These performance capabilities help maintain consistent operation.

Documentation tools support solution maintenance. Technical documentation describes system operation. Integration documentation guides system connection. Maintenance documentation supports ongoing operation. These documentation capabilities help maintain system knowledge.

Version control tools manage development progress. Code management tracks system changes. Asset versioning maintains content organization. Release management enables systematic deployment. These version control capabilities help maintain reliable development.

Quality assurance tools verify system reliability. Automated testing confirms system operation. Performance validation ensures consistent behavior. Balance testing verifies fair gameplay. These quality capabilities help maintain effective solutions.

Deployment tools support system distribution. Build management creates release versions. Distribution systems enable efficient delivery. Update management maintains current versions. These deployment capabilities help maintain effective distribution.

Analytics tools measure system performance. Player behavior analysis tracks engagement. Performance metrics verify system operation. Resource utilization ensures efficient operation. These analytics capabilities help maintain effective solutions.

Security tools protect system operation. Input validation prevents exploitation. State verification maintains fair play. Anti-cheat systems protect competitive balance. These security capabilities help maintain reliable operation.

Configuration tools manage system settings. Game parameters maintain appropriate challenge. AI behavior configuration enables customization. Performance settings optimize operation. These configuration capabilities help create effective solutions.

Optimization tools improve system performance. Code optimization enhances processing efficiency. Resource management ensures efficient usage. Network optimization reduces latency. These optimization capabilities help maintain reliable operation.

Content management tools organize game assets. Model management maintains AI components. Visual asset organization enables efficient access. Audio content management supports immersion. These management capabilities help maintain effective operation.

Community tools support development efforts. Knowledge sharing enables problem resolution. Asset sharing accelerates development. Experience sharing guides implementation. These community capabilities help maintain development effectiveness.

Training tools support development preparation. Tutorial systems explain tool capabilities. Practice environments enable safe learning. Reference materials provide ongoing support. These training capabilities help prepare for effective tool usage.

The evolution of gaming tools continues through careful advancement. New capabilities emerge through validated development. Implementation options expand with experience. These developments create new possibilities while maintaining development reliability.

The practical applications of Gaming AI solutions

demonstrate their transformative impact across various gaming domains. Understanding these applications helps developers identify implementation opportunities while providing concrete examples of successful deployment.

Game world generation represents a fundamental application area. Procedural terrain generation creates diverse landscapes. Building generation develops varied structures. Population systems place appropriate objects. Environment management maintains consistent worlds. These applications demonstrate how AI enhances world creation while maintaining performance standards.

Character behavior systems implement sophisticated interactions. Non-player character AI maintains believable behavior. Crowd simulation creates realistic group movement. Enemy AI provides appropriate challenge. Companion AI offers meaningful assistance. These applications show how AI enhances character interaction while maintaining game balance.

Strategic decision-making systems enable sophisticated gameplay. Resource management AI optimizes usage decisions. Combat AI implements tactical choices. Diplomatic AI manages relationship systems. Economic AI handles trading decisions. These applications demonstrate how AI creates engaging strategic challenges.

Player interaction systems enhance gaming experiences. Dialog systems enable natural conversation. Quest generation creates meaningful objectives. Tutorial systems provide appropriate guidance. Difficulty adaptation maintains engagement. These applications show how AI enhances player experience while maintaining appropriate challenge.

Environmental response systems create dynamic worlds. Weather systems implement atmospheric changes. Ecosystem simulation maintains environmental balance. Day-night cycles affect game behavior. Season changes influence gameplay elements. These applications demonstrate how AI creates living worlds.

211

Movement systems enable realistic motion. Path-finding implements efficient navigation. Obstacle avoidance prevents unrealistic collision. Formation management coordinates group movement. Animation blending creates smooth transitions. These applications show how AI enhances motion quality.

Combat systems implement engaging challenges. Tactical positioning enables strategic combat. Attack pattern generation creates varied challenges. Defense behavior implements appropriate responses. Damage calculation maintains fair interaction. These applications demonstrate how AI creates balanced combat.

Resource management systems optimize game operation. Memory allocation maintains efficient usage. Processing distribution ensures balanced load. Network utilization optimizes multiplayer interaction. Asset streaming manages content delivery. These applications show how AI enhances operational efficiency.

Learning systems enable gameplay adaptation. Strategy refinement improves AI decisions. Pattern recognition identifies player approaches. Difficulty adjustment maintains appropriate challenge. Performance optimization enhances operation. These applications demonstrate how AI creates evolving experiences.

Quest systems generate engaging content. Story generation maintains narrative consistency. Mission creation ensures meaningful objectives. Reward balancing maintains player motivation. Progress tracking enables advancement. These applications show how AI enhances game content.

Social systems implement character interaction. Relationship modeling tracks character connections. Conversation generation creates natural dialog. Emotional response simulates realistic reactions. Group behavior coordinates multiple characters. These applications demonstrate how AI creates believable social environments.

Economic systems manage game resources. Market

simulation implements realistic trading. Price adjustment maintains economic balance. Resource distribution creates meaningful choices. Currency management prevents inflation. These applications show how AI enhances economic gameplay.

Physics systems maintain realistic interaction. Object behavior simulates appropriate motion. Environmental effects create realistic responses. Particle systems generate visual effects. Collision handling prevents unrealistic interaction. These applications demonstrate how AI enhances physical realism.

Audio systems create immersive environments. Sound generation produces appropriate effects. Music adaptation responds to gameplay. Environmental audio maintains atmosphere. Voice generation creates character dialog. These applications show how AI enhances audio experiences.

Testing systems verify game operation. Performance validation ensures consistent operation. Balance testing confirms fair gameplay. Integration testing verifies system coordination. Player testing validates engagement. These applications demonstrate how AI supports development.

Analysis systems measure game effectiveness. Player behavior analysis tracks engagement. Performance monitoring ensures efficient operation. Balance assessment verifies fair play. These applications show how AI enhances game understanding.

Security systems protect game integrity. Anti-cheat measures prevent exploitation. State verification maintains fair play. Monitoring identifies unusual behavior. These applications demonstrate how AI maintains game reliability.

Management systems support ongoing operation. Version control tracks system changes. Asset management maintains content organization. Player management handles user data. These applications show how AI enhances operational effectiveness.

The evolution of gaming applications continues through

careful advancement. New capabilities emerge through validated development. Implementation options expand with experience. These developments create new possibilities while maintaining operational reliability.

The future of Gaming AI solutions continues to evolve through careful advancement of both technological capabilities and player experience enhancement. Understanding emerging trends and potential developments helps organizations prepare for future capabilities while maintaining current operational standards.

Performance optimization continues to advance through various developments. Enhanced processing enables more complex AI behavior. Improved resource management supports larger game worlds. Advanced network optimization reduces latency impact. These improvements may enhance gaming experiences while maintaining reliable operation.

Character interaction promises enhanced sophistication. Improved natural language processing enables more realistic dialogue. Advanced behavior modeling creates more believable characters. Enhanced emotional simulation provides deeper interactions. These developments may improve character engagement while maintaining performance requirements.

World generation capabilities continue to expand. Enhanced procedural generation creates more diverse environments. Improved asset creation enables richer content. Advanced physics simulation provides more realistic interaction. These developments may enhance world complexity while maintaining operational efficiency.

Learning systems are becoming more sophisticated. Enhanced strategy adaptation improves AI responses. Advanced pattern recognition enables better player understanding. Improved difficulty adjustment maintains appropriate challenge. These developments may enhance gameplay evolution while maintaining fair competition.

Integration capabilities expand through standardization

214

efforts. Enhanced protocols enable better system connection. Improved data exchange supports comprehensive operation. Standardized interfaces simplify implementation. These advances may improve system integration while maintaining reliability.

Resource management is advancing through new approaches. Enhanced memory optimization improves efficiency. Advanced processing distribution enables better performance. Improved asset streaming supports larger worlds. These developments may enhance resource usage while maintaining reliable operation.

Quality assurance is advancing through refined methods. Enhanced testing verifies operation more thoroughly. Advanced validation confirms reliability better. Improved monitoring tracks performance more effectively. These developments may improve quality while maintaining efficiency.

Security measures are advancing with emerging threats. Enhanced protection prevents exploitation better. Advanced monitoring identifies issues more effectively. Improved response handles security incidents better. These developments may strengthen security while maintaining playability.

Development tools are becoming more sophisticated. Enhanced creation tools improve efficiency. Advanced testing enables better validation. Improved deployment simplifies distribution. These developments may enhance development while maintaining reliability.

Player analysis is advancing through new capabilities. Enhanced behavior tracking provides better understanding. Advanced performance monitoring ensures consistent operation. Improved feedback analysis guides development better. These developments may improve player experience while maintaining privacy.

Content generation is evolving through new approaches. Enhanced asset creation enables more variety. Advanced story generation provides better narratives. Improved quest development creates meaningful objectives. These developments may enhance content while maintaining consistency.

Multiplayer systems are advancing through improved technology. Enhanced synchronization reduces latency effects. Advanced matchmaking provides better game balance. Improved social features enable better interaction. These developments may enhance multiplayer while maintaining fairness.

Performance optimization continues through various approaches. Enhanced processing improves operational efficiency. Advanced resource usage optimizes system operation. Improved monitoring guides optimization efforts. These developments may improve performance while maintaining reliability.

Documentation systems are evolving to support complexity. Enhanced technical recording maintains system knowledge. Advanced operational logging tracks performance better. Improved maintenance tracking guides service more effectively. These developments may improve system management while maintaining clarity.

Training approaches are evolving to meet changing needs. Enhanced tutorials provide better guidance. Advanced practice modes improve skill development. Improved feedback helps player improvement. These developments may enhance learning while maintaining engagement.

Community features are advancing through new capabilities. Enhanced social interaction supports player connection. Advanced content sharing enables better collaboration. Improved communication tools support player interaction. These developments may enhance community while maintaining appropriate boundaries.

Implementation practices continue to mature. Enhanced planning improves deployment success. Advanced integration simplifies connection. Improved management ensures reliable operation. These developments may improve implementation while maintaining standards.

Future possibilities are emerging through ongoing research. New capabilities advance through careful validation. Implementation options expand with experience. These developments may create new opportunities while maintaining essential standards.

The evolution suggests continuing advancement in capabilities, implementation approaches, and operational practices. Organizations must maintain awareness of these developments while planning current implementations to ensure sustainable, effective solutions.

Our exploration of Gaming AI solutions has revealed how artificial intelligence enables sophisticated interactive experiences while maintaining essential performance and engagement standards. From examining fundamental principles of game AI to investigating practical applications, we've established a comprehensive foundation for implementing these technologies within the unique requirements of gaming environments.

The principles we've explored regarding real-time processing, player interaction, and dynamic content generation demonstrate how AI implementations must adapt to the demands of creating engaging virtual experiences. These lessons prove particularly valuable as we move forward to examine Cross-Domain AI Projects, where multiple AI capabilities must work together cohesively to create comprehensive solutions that span different application areas.

The implementation considerations we've examined, from resource requirements and performance optimization to integration needs and player experience management, provide valuable context for understanding how organizations deploy sophisticated AI solutions. While specific technologies may differ, the fundamental principles of successful AI implementation persist. This understanding will prove particularly valuable as we examine how organizations combine different AI capabilities to create solutions that leverage multiple domains of artificial intelligence.

The relationship between Gaming AI and Cross-Domain projects illustrates important parallels in system integration and coordination. Where gaming systems must coordinate multiple AI capabilities within virtual environments, cross-domain projects must orchestrate various AI technologies across different application areas. Understanding these parallels helps organizations implement comprehensive solutions that maintain appropriate standards across multiple domains.

Our journey continues as we examine how organizations implement Cross-Domain AI Projects that combine various AI capabilities to create sophisticated solutions. This transition from Gaming AI to Cross-Domain projects represents more than a shift in scope, it demonstrates how artificial intelligence technologies can work together to create capabilities greater than the sum of their parts while maintaining essential requirements for reliable and effective operation.

The path ahead reveals how organizations leverage multiple AI domains in combination, creating solutions that demonstrate the full potential of artificial intelligence working in concert. This exploration will further expand our understanding of AI's practical implementation possibilities while maintaining focus on essential requirements for comprehensive and reliable operation.

CHAPTER 10: CROSS-DOMAIN AI PROJECTS

Our exploration of artificial intelligence solutions now enters the sophisticated realm of cross-domain integration, where multiple AI capabilities work together to create comprehensive solutions. Having examined individual domains from language processing to gaming systems, we now investigate how these technologies combine to create solutions greater than the sum of their parts. Consider DeepMind's AlphaFold 2, which revolutionized protein structure prediction by combining deep learning, molecular biology understanding, and evolutionary analysis into a single system that achieved breakthrough accuracy of over 90% in protein structure prediction.

The evolution of cross-domain AI projects represents a significant advancement in artificial intelligence applications. From early attempts at combining basic capabilities to today's sophisticated systems, these implementations demonstrate both the remarkable potential of combined AI technologies and the crucial importance of maintaining effective coordination between different components. For instance,

OpenAI's GPT-4V (formerly GPT-4 with vision) exemplifies this evolution, seamlessly integrating advanced language understanding with sophisticated visual processing to analyze images, create detailed descriptions, and engage in natural language dialogue about visual content.

The implementation of cross-domain projects involves unique considerations that distinguish them from single-domain solutions. Integration between different AI capabilities demands careful coordination while maintaining performance across all components. Tesla's Full Self-Driving (FSD) system demonstrates these challenges, combining computer vision for environmental perception, natural language processing for user interaction, and sophisticated decision-making algorithms for vehicle control. The system processes inputs from eight cameras, twelve ultrasonic sensors, and forward-facing radar, coordinating these diverse data streams to enable autonomous driving capabilities.

The relationship between different AI domains proves particularly significant in these implementations. Language processing might provide user interaction while vision systems analyze environmental information. Google's LaMDA (Language Model for Dialogue Applications) showcases this integration by combining natural language understanding with extensive knowledge graphs and multi-modal processing capabilities. Similarly, Amazon's Alexa multimodal AI system demonstrates how voice recognition, natural language understanding, and visual processing can work together, enabling users to interact through speech while the system processes both verbal and visual inputs to provide more contextually relevant responses.

As we begin our examination of cross-domain AI projects, we'll explore how organizations implement these comprehensive solutions while maintaining performance and reliability across multiple AI domains. Meta's PyTorch framework exemplifies the tools enabling these integrations, providing a unified platform where developers can seamlessly combine computer vision, natural language processing, and other AI capabilities. From understanding fundamental principles of domain integration to examining specific implementation approaches, our journey reveals how organizations combine AI capabilities to create sophisticated solutions that leverage the strengths of different domains while maintaining essential operational standards.

Cross-domain AI solutions operate under unique principles that combine multiple artificial intelligence capabilities while maintaining coordinated operation. Understanding these fundamentals proves essential for implementing solutions that effectively integrate different AI domains while maintaining reliable performance. For example, NVIDIA's Omniverse platform demonstrates these principles in action, providing a universal framework where AI models for physics simulation, computer vision, and natural language processing work together in real-time.

Integration architectures form the foundation of cross-domain implementations. System designs must support communication between different AI components. The Hugging Face Transformers library exemplifies this architectural approach, providing a unified framework that enables seamless integration of various AI models, from BERT for language understanding to ViT for computer vision tasks. Data flow patterns need to accommodate various processing requirements. Resource management must coordinate multiple subsystems. These architectural considerations help create reliable combined solutions.

Communication frameworks enable component interaction. Apache Kafka, widely deployed in enterprise AI systems, illustrates how standard protocols support data exchange between domains. Modern implementations like Confluent Cloud demonstrate how message formats maintain consistent information transfer across complex AI systems. State management tracks system conditions through tools like Redis, which maintains real-time synchronization across distributed AI components. These communication capabilities help maintain coordinated operation.

Resource management ensures reliable operation across domains. Kubernetes, the industry standard for container orchestration, shows how processing allocation balances computational needs in large-scale AI deployments. Memory management coordinates storage requirements through systems like Apache Ignite, which provides distributed memory management for AI applications. Network resources support distributed operation through frameworks like Ray, which enables efficient scaling of cross-domain AI applications. These resource considerations help maintain efficient system function.

Performance monitoring tracks operation across components. Tools like Prometheus and Grafana demonstrate how response time measurement verifies timely interaction in production AI systems. Resource utilization monitors system efficiency through platforms like Datadog, which provides comprehensive monitoring of AI infrastructure. Quality metrics track operational reliability using systems like MLflow, which enables detailed tracking of model performance. These monitoring systems help maintain consistent operation.

State synchronization maintains system coordination. Examples like Apache ZooKeeper show how component status tracking ensures aligned operation in distributed AI systems. Event management coordinates system responses through tools like RabbitMQ, which enables reliable message queuing and event processing. Transaction management maintains operational consistency using frameworks like Apache Flink for stream processing. These synchronization capabilities help maintain reliable function.

Error handling implements multiple response levels. Modern platforms like Sentry demonstrate how component errors require appropriate isolation in AI systems. System errors need coordinated recovery through tools like Istio, which provides sophisticated service mesh capabilities for error handling. Integration errors demand careful resolution through frameworks like Apache Airflow, which manages complex AI workflows. These error handling capabilities help maintain reliable operation.

Quality assurance implements comprehensive validation. Popular frameworks like PyTest showcase how component testing verifies individual operation in AI systems. Integration testing confirms coordinated function through tools like Jenkins, which automates testing pipelines. System testing validates complete operation using platforms like GitLab CI/CD. These quality measures help maintain reliable solutions.

Security implementation protects multiple domains. Leading tools like HashiCorp Vault demonstrate how access control manages component interaction in AI systems. Data protection ensures secure transfer through frameworks like Apache Knox. Operation monitoring identifies potential issues using platforms like Elastic Security. These security measures help maintain safe operation.

Documentation requirements reflect system complexity. Modern platforms like Confluence exemplify how architecture documentation describes system structure. Integration documentation guides component connection through tools like Swagger for API documentation. Operation documentation supports system management using platforms like GitBook. These documentation practices help maintain system knowledge.

Testing protocols verify coordinated operation. Frameworks like Robot Framework show how unit testing validates component function in AI systems. Integration testing confirms domain interaction through tools like Selenium for automated testing. System testing verifies complete operation using platforms like JMeter for performance testing. These testing approaches help maintain reliable solutions.

Core integration models represent fundamental

approaches to combining multiple AI domains into cohesive solutions. Understanding these models and their capabilities proves essential for effective implementation of cross-domain projects. Microsoft's Azure Cognitive Services exemplifies this approach, providing a comprehensive platform that integrates vision, language, speech, and decision-making capabilities through standardized APIs and services.

Communication frameworks establish reliable interaction patterns. Google's Protocol Buffers demonstrates how message-based systems enable asynchronous operation between domains, being widely used in production systems like TensorFlow Serving. Event-driven architectures support reactive coordination, as shown by AWS EventBridge which enables sophisticated event routing between AI services. Service-oriented approaches provide structured interaction, exemplified by gRPC's high-performance RPC framework used in distributed AI systems. These frameworks help maintain reliable communication while enabling efficient integration.

Data exchange models support information transfer. Apache Arrow, adopted by major data science platforms, shows how standardized formats ensure consistent understanding across different AI components. Translation layers convert between domain requirements, as demonstrated by NVIDIA's RAPIDS which enables seamless conversion between CPU and GPU data formats. Apache Parquet provides validation systems that verify data integrity in large-scale AI operations. These exchange capabilities help maintain reliable information flow while preserving data quality.

State management models coordinate system conditions. Etcd, used in Kubernetes clusters, exemplifies how distributed state tracking maintains system awareness in complex AI deployments. Synchronization protocols ensure consistent operation, as demonstrated by Apache ZooKeeper's coordination services in distributed AI systems. Redis Sentinel shows how recovery mechanisms handle state inconsistencies in production environments. These management capabilities help maintain reliable operation while enabling system coordination.

Resource coordination models optimize system usage. Kubernetes' scheduling system demonstrates how load balancing distributes processing demands across AI workloads. Memory management coordinates storage requirements through systems like Apache Ignite's distributed memory architecture. NVIDIA's Multi-Instance GPU technology optimizes network utilization for AI workloads. These coordination capabilities help maintain efficient operation while enabling effective resource use.

Performance balancing models maintain system efficiency. Google's Borg scheduler shows how processing allocation ensures fair resource distribution in large-scale AI systems. Priority management handles competing demands through tools like Apache Mesos, which provides sophisticated resource allocation for AI workloads. Nomad by HashiCorp demonstrates how scheduling systems coordinate operations across diverse AI workloads. These balancing capabilities help maintain consistent performance while enabling effective operation.

Error handling models manage system issues. Circuit breakers implemented in tools like Istio show how component isolation prevents error propagation in AI systems. Recovery coordination ensures systematic response through platforms like Consul, which provides service mesh capabilities. Netflix's Hystrix library demonstrates state restoration maintains system integrity in distributed AI applications. These handling capabilities help maintain reliable operation while enabling effective problem resolution.

Quality assurance models verify system operation. JUnit's testing framework shows how component validation ensures reliable function in AI systems. Integration testing confirms proper coordination through tools like TestNG for complex AI workflows. Selenium enables system verification validates complete operation across distributed components. These assurance capabilities help maintain reliable solutions while enabling effective validation.

Integration frameworks support system development. Apache Airflow demonstrates how component connection maintains coordinated operation in AI pipelines. Resource management ensures efficient function through tools like Apache Yarn in distributed environments. MLflow shows how error handling provides reliable recovery in machine learning workflows. These framework capabilities help create effective solutions while enabling reliable implementation.

Documentation models maintain system knowledge. Swagger/OpenAPI specifications demonstrate how architecture documentation describes system structure in AI services. Integration documentation guides component connection through tools like ReadTheDocs used in major AI frameworks. GitBook shows how operation documentation supports system management across complex AI deployments. These documentation capabilities help maintain system understanding while enabling effective maintenance.

Testing models verify system operation. PyTest frameworks demonstrate unit testing validates component function in AI systems. Integration testing confirms domain interaction through tools like Robot Framework for automated testing. Locust enables system testing verifies complete operation under load. These testing capabilities help maintain reliable solutions while enabling effective verification.

Performance optimization models improve system efficiency. NVIDIA TensorRT shows how processing optimization enhances operational speed in AI inference. Resource optimization ensures efficient usage through tools like Intel's OpenVINO toolkit. gRPC demonstrates how communication optimization reduces transfer overhead in distributed AI systems. These optimization capabilities help maintain effective operation while enabling efficient function.

Security models protect system operation. HashiCorp Vault demonstrates how access management controls component interaction in AI deployments. Data protection ensures secure transfer through tools like Apache Knox. Elastic Security shows how operation monitoring identifies potential issues across AI infrastructure. These security capabilities help maintain safe operation while enabling effective protection.

Multi-domain processing represents the practical implementation of combining different AI capabilities into cohesive operations. Understanding these processing approaches proves essential for creating effective cross-domain solutions. OpenAI's GPT-4V exemplifies this integration, combining sophisticated language understanding with visual processing capabilities to enable natural interactions with both text and images.

Language-vision integration combines natural language and visual processing capabilities. Google's PaLM-E demonstrates how text analysis provides context for image understanding in robotics applications. Microsoft's Florence foundation model shows how visual information enhances language comprehension through multimodal learning. Meta's CM3leon reveals how combined analysis enables richer interpretation by processing both visual and textual information simultaneously. These integration capabilities help create comprehensive understanding while maintaining processing efficiency.

Vision-robotics coordination enables sophisticated physical interaction. Boston Dynamics' Atlas robot demonstrates how visual analysis guides robotic movement in complex environments. Tesla's Optimus platform shows how spatial understanding enables precise navigation through computer vision and sensor fusion. Amazon's warehouse robots illustrate how object recognition supports manipulation tasks in production environments. These coordination capabilities help create effective physical

227

operation while maintaining safe interaction.

Data-language processing combines analytical and communication capabilities. IBM Watson Discovery reveals how data analysis informs language generation in enterprise applications. Salesforce Einstein demonstrates how natural language queries enable data exploration across complex datasets. Databricks' Dolly shows how results presentation provides clear communication of analytical insights. These processing capabilities help create meaningful insights while maintaining clear understanding.

Audio-visual systems implement synchronized media processing. Google's YouTube Speech-Text Enhanced shows how speech analysis coordinates with visual recognition for improved captioning. NVIDIA Maxine demonstrates how sound localization enhances spatial understanding in video conferencing. Meta's AudioCraft illustrates how combined processing enables rich media interpretation and generation. These system capabilities help create comprehensive media analysis while maintaining temporal alignment.

Multi-modal analysis implements coordinated processing across domains. DeepMind's Flamingo model shows how input correlation identifies related information across modalities. Anthropic's Claude demonstrates how cross-domain validation enhances accuracy in complex tasks. Google's Gemini reveals how combined interpretation enables deeper understanding of diverse inputs. These analysis capabilities help create comprehensive insights while maintaining processing reliability.

Combined decision making leverages multiple information sources. Waymo's autonomous driving platform shows how cross-domain analysis informs real-time choices. Tesla's Autopilot demonstrates how multiple perspectives enhance evaluation of driving conditions. Aurora's self-driving system illustrates how coordinated processing supports complex decisions. These decision capabilities help create effective choices while maintaining analytical reliability.

Integrated response systems coordinate multiple outputs. Amazon's Alexa demonstrates how response selection considers domain requirements across modalities. Apple's Siri shows how output coordination maintains consistency in multimodal interactions. Google Assistant reveals how delivery timing ensures appropriate sequence of responses. These response capabilities help create effective interaction while maintaining system coordination.

Resource management optimizes multi-domain operation. Kubernetes demonstrates how processing allocation balances domain needs in production environments. Apache Spark shows how memory management coordinates storage requirements for distributed AI workloads. Ray exemplifies how network utilization optimizes communication in multi-agent systems. These management capabilities help maintain efficient operation while enabling effective coordination.

Performance monitoring tracks cross-domain operation. Prometheus illustrates how response time measurement verifies coordination in production systems. Grafana demonstrates how resource utilization monitors efficiency across AI workloads. Datadog shows how quality metrics track reliability in distributed environments. These monitoring capabilities help maintain consistent operation while enabling performance optimization.

Error handling manages cross-domain issues. Istio service mesh shows how domain isolation prevents error propagation in production systems. Apache Airflow demonstrates how recovery coordination ensures systematic response in AI pipelines. HashiCorp's Consul reveals how state restoration maintains system integrity across services. These handling capabilities help maintain reliable operation while enabling effective problem resolution.

Quality assurance verifies multi-domain operation. MLflow demonstrates how domain validation ensures reliable function in production environments. Jenkins shows how integration testing confirms coordination across AI systems.

GitLab CI/CD reveals how system verification validates complete operation of complex deployments. These assurance capabilities help maintain reliable solutions while enabling effective validation.

Security implementation protects cross-domain operation. HashiCorp Vault shows how access control manages domain interaction in production environments. Apache Knox demonstrates how data protection ensures secure transfer between components. Elastic Security reveals how operation monitoring identifies issues across distributed systems. These security capabilities help maintain safe operation while enabling effective protection.

The implementation of cross-domain AI solutions demands attention to unique considerations that combine multiple domain requirements with integrated operation needs. Understanding these considerations helps ensure successful deployment while maintaining reliable operation across all domains. Microsoft Azure's AI infrastructure demonstrates these principles, showing how careful planning and robust architecture support complex AI deployments at scale.

System requirements address multiple domain needs. Google Cloud's AI Platform shows how computing resources must support combined processing demands across diverse workloads. Amazon S3 demonstrates how storage capacity needs accommodate multiple data types in production environments. NVIDIA's DGX systems reveal how network infrastructure requires appropriate bandwidth and latency for AI workloads. Tesla's Dojo supercomputer illustrates how power systems need adequate capacity for intensive AI operations. These requirements help create reliable operational environments.

Integration planning ensures practical coordination. Kubernetes' orchestration capabilities demonstrate how domain connection maintains efficient operation at scale. Apache Kafka shows how data flow enables appropriate information exchange between services. AWS Resource Groups reveal how resource sharing supports combined function across services. GitLab's project management tools illustrate how timeline management coordinates implementation effectively. These planning considerations help create effective solutions.

Performance management implements comprehensive monitoring. Datadog's observability platform demonstrates how response time tracking verifies timely operation in production. Grafana's dashboards show how resource utilization monitors system efficiency across components. Prometheus metrics reveal how quality metrics track operational reliability. Google's Cloud Load Balancing illustrates how load distribution ensures balanced operation. These management practices help maintain reliable function.

Resource allocation optimizes system operation. OpenShift's container platform shows how processing distribution balances computational needs effectively. Redis Enterprise demonstrates how memory assignment coordinates storage requirements across services. Cloudflare's network services reveal how network resources support distributed operation. NVIDIA's CUDA demonstrates how power management ensures adequate supply for GPU operations. These allocation practices help maintain efficient operation.

Quality standards establish operational requirements. ISO/IEC 25010 software quality standards show how performance criteria define response expectations. AWS's Well-Architected Framework demonstrates how reliability standards specify uptime requirements. Google's SRE practices reveal how accuracy metrics establish precision needs. Microsoft's Azure Architecture Center illustrates how integration quality defines coordination requirements. These standards help maintain reliable operation.

Testing protocols verify system operation. PyTest frameworks show how component testing validates domain function effectively. Jenkins demonstrates how integration testing confirms coordination across services. JMeter reveals how system testing verifies complete operation under load. Selenium illustrates how user testing validates practical utility. These protocols help maintain reliable solutions.

Security implementation protects multiple domains. AWS IAM shows how access control manages system usage effectively. HashiCorp Vault demonstrates how data protection ensures secure transfer between services. Elastic Security reveals how operation monitoring identifies potential issues. PagerDuty illustrates how incident response handles security events effectively. These security measures help maintain safe operation.

Documentation requirements span multiple areas. Confluence demonstrates how architecture documentation describes system structure clearly. Swagger/OpenAPI shows how integration documentation guides domain connection. GitBook reveals how operation documentation supports system management. ReadTheDocs illustrates how maintenance documentation enables ongoing support. These documentation practices help maintain system knowledge.

Performance optimization ensures reliable operation. TensorRT shows how code optimization improves processing efficiency in AI workloads. Intel's OpenVINO demonstrates how memory management maintains efficient resource usage. gRPC reveals how network optimization reduces communication overhead. NVIDIA's CUDA illustrates how power optimization ensures efficient energy use. These optimization approaches help maintain consistent operation.

Error handling implements multiple responses. Circuit breaker patterns in Istio show how domain errors require appropriate isolation. Consul demonstrates how system errors need coordinated recovery across services. Apache Airflow reveals how integration errors demand careful resolution. PagerDuty illustrates how operation errors require systematic response. These error handling capabilities help maintain reliable operation.

Version management maintains system currency. GitLab demonstrates how update procedures keep domains current effectively. Jenkins shows how testing processes verify changes across components. ArgoCD reveals how rollback capabilities ensure reliability in deployments. JFrog Artifactory illustrates how distribution systems enable efficient delivery. These management practices help maintain effective solutions.

Asset management supports system operation. MLflow shows how model management maintains AI components effectively. MinIO demonstrates how data organization enables efficient access across services. Terraform reveals how resource tracking supports system operation. Ansible illustrates how configuration management maintains settings reliably. These management practices help maintain effective operation.

Cross-domain tools transform theoretical integration capabilities into practical solutions, enabling organizations to implement sophisticated multi-domain AI systems while maintaining reliable operation. Understanding these tools proves crucial for effective implementation. The Hugging Face ecosystem exemplifies this transformation, providing comprehensive tools for developing, training, and deploying various AI models across domains.

Integration frameworks support combined domain implementation. PyTorch demonstrates how communication libraries enable reliable domain interaction through its distributed computing capabilities. Apache Arrow shows how data exchange tools support information transfer between different AI frameworks. Redis Enterprise reveals how state management maintains system coordination in production environments. Kubernetes illustrates how resource management optimizes system usage across complex deployments. These framework capabilities help create effective solutions.

Development platforms enable cross-domain creation.

Visual Studio Code with its AI extensions shows how integrated development environments support multi-domain coding effectively. JupyterLab demonstrates how interactive development supports AI experimentation and development. GitLab reveals how version control and CI/CD pipelines enable systematic development. PyCharm Professional illustrates how specialized IDE features support AI development workflows. These platform capabilities help maintain development efficiency.

Testing tools verify cross-domain operation. PyTest frameworks show how integration testing confirms domain coordination in AI systems. Locust demonstrates how performance testing ensures reliable operation under load. OWASP ZAP reveals how security testing validates protection measures effectively. Selenium illustrates how user testing verifies practical utility in production environments. These testing capabilities help maintain reliable solutions.

Monitoring tools track multi-domain performance. Prometheus exhibits how response time tracking verifies timely operation in production systems. Grafana demonstrates how resource utilization monitors system efficiency across components. Datadog reveals how quality metrics track operational reliability comprehensively. New Relic illustrates how application performance monitoring ensures system health. These monitoring capabilities help maintain effective operation.

Management tools support ongoing operation. GitLab shows how version control tracks system changes systematically. Ansible demonstrates how configuration management maintains settings across environments. Terraform reveals how infrastructure management enables consistent deployment. Harbor illustrates how container registry management supports efficient distribution. These management capabilities help maintain reliable solutions.

Documentation tools support solution maintenance. Confluence demonstrates how architecture documentation describes system structure effectively. Swagger/OpenAPI shows how API documentation guides integration efforts. GitBook reveals how user documentation supports system utilization. ReadTheDocs illustrates how technical documentation maintains development knowledge. These documentation capabilities help maintain system knowledge.

Quality assurance tools verify system reliability. Jenkins shows how automated testing confirms system operation consistently. JMeter demonstrates how performance validation ensures consistent behavior. SonarQube reveals how code quality analysis maintains development standards. Selenium Grid illustrates how distributed testing enables comprehensive validation. These quality capabilities help maintain effective solutions.

Deployment tools support system distribution. ArgoCD shows how continuous deployment manages production releases. Docker demonstrates how containerization enables consistent environment management. Helm reveals how package management streamlines Kubernetes deployments. Spinnaker illustrates how multi-cloud deployment enables flexible distribution. These deployment capabilities help maintain effective distribution.

Analytics tools measure system performance. Elastic APM shows how performance metrics verify system operation comprehensively. Grafana demonstrates how resource utilization ensures efficient operation. Kibana reveals how log analysis guides system optimization. Datadog illustrates how user interaction analysis informs improvements. These analytics capabilities help maintain effective solutions.

Security tools protect multi-domain operation. HashiCorp Vault shows how access control manages system usage securely. Apache Knox demonstrates how data protection ensures secure transfer. Elastic Security reveals how operation monitoring identifies threats effectively. PagerDuty illustrates how incident response handles security events systematically. These security capabilities help maintain safe operation.

Configuration tools manage system settings. Ansible shows how domain parameters maintain appropriate operation across environments. Terraform demonstrates how infrastructure configuration enables consistent deployment. Puppet reveals how system configuration maintains operational standards. Chef illustrates how automation ensures reliable configuration management. These configuration capabilities help create effective solutions.

Optimization tools improve system performance. NVIDIA TensorRT shows how code optimization enhances processing efficiency. Intel OpenVINO demonstrates how hardware acceleration improves performance. Apache TVM reveals how deep learning compilation optimizes model execution. ONNX Runtime illustrates how inference optimization enables efficient deployment. These optimization capabilities help maintain reliable operation.

The practical applications of cross-domain AI solutions demonstrate their transformative impact across various implementation scenarios. Understanding these applications helps organizations identify integration opportunities while providing concrete examples of successful deployment. The healthcare sector exemplifies this through systems like Google DeepMind's AlphaFold 2, which combines multiple AI domains to predict protein structures with unprecedented accuracy.

Combined systems implement multiple domain capabilities. Meta's LLaMA 2 demonstrates how language-vision systems enable natural interaction with visual content through multimodal processing. Boston Dynamics' Atlas shows how vision-robotics integration supports physical interaction through visual guidance. Bloomberg's AI financial analysis platform reveals how data-language solutions combine analysis with natural communication for market insights. These applications demonstrate how domain combination enhances overall capabilities.

Integrated solutions leverage complementary strengths.

Waymo's autonomous driving platform shows how analytical-interactive systems combine data processing with real-time decision making. Apple's Siri demonstrates how sensory-processing solutions merge multiple input types for comprehensive understanding. IBM Watson for Oncology reveals how decision-support systems integrate multiple analysis approaches for medical diagnosis. These implementations show how domain integration creates enhanced functionality.

Multi-modal applications process various input types. Microsoft Teams Premium shows how audio-visual processing enables comprehensive meeting analysis and transcription. Google Translate's camera feature demonstrates how text-speech systems support natural communication methods. Tesla's Autopilot reveals how gesture-voice solutions enable intuitive vehicle interaction. These applications demonstrate how multiple input processing enhances user experience.

Performance analysis implements comprehensive monitoring. Amazon's AWS CloudWatch shows how cross-domain metrics track combined operation in cloud environments. Datadog's unified monitoring demonstrates how integration effectiveness measures coordination quality. Google Cloud's operations suite reveals how resource utilization monitors system efficiency at scale. These analysis applications help maintain operational reliability.

Quality management ensures reliable operation. Microsoft's Azure DevOps shows how integration validation verifies domain coordination in production. GitLab's CI/CD pipeline demonstrates how performance monitoring tracks system behavior systematically. New Relic's observability platform reveals how user experience assessment guides improvements effectively. These maintenance applications help maintain solution effectiveness.

Resource optimization supports efficient operation. Kubernetes shows how processing distribution balances computational loads across clusters. Redis Enterprise demonstrates how memory management coordinates storage usage effectively. Cloudflare's edge computing network reveals how network utilization optimizes communication paths globally. These optimization applications help maintain system efficiency.

System monitoring tracks operational status. Prometheus demonstrates how performance metrics verify timely response in production environments. Grafana's dashboards show how resource usage monitors utilization patterns comprehensively. Elastic Stack reveals how quality measures track reliability levels across distributed systems. These monitoring applications help maintain operational awareness.

Maintenance procedures support ongoing operation. MLflow shows how update management maintains current capabilities in AI systems. Jenkins demonstrates how integration verification ensures continued coordination. Apache Airflow reveals how performance optimization improves system efficiency in data pipelines. These maintenance applications help maintain reliable function.

Security implementation protects system operation. HashiCorp Vault demonstrates how access control manages component interaction securely. AWS KMS shows how data protection ensures secure transfer across services. Elastic Security reveals how operation monitoring identifies potential issues proactively. These security applications help maintain safe operation.

Documentation systems maintain solution knowledge. Confluence shows how architecture documentation describes system structure comprehensively. Swagger/OpenAPI demonstrates how integration documentation guides domain connection effectively. GitBook reveals how operation documentation supports system management reliably. These documentation applications help maintain system understanding.

Testing applications verify system operation. PyTest

frameworks show how integration testing confirms domain coordination systematically. JMeter demonstrates how performance testing ensures reliable operation under load. OWASP ZAP reveals how security testing validates protection measures thoroughly. These testing applications help maintain solution reliability.

Development support enables efficient creation. Visual Studio Code shows how integration frameworks support domain combination effectively. JupyterLab demonstrates how testing tools verify system operation interactively. GitHub Actions reveals how deployment systems enable distribution systematically. These support applications help maintain development effectiveness.

The future of cross-domain AI solutions continues to evolve through careful advancement of both integration capabilities and practical applications. Understanding emerging trends and potential developments helps organizations prepare for future capabilities while maintaining current operational standards. Google's Gemini Ultra demonstrates this evolution, showing how next-generation models can seamlessly integrate multiple modalities with unprecedented capabilities.

Integration capabilities promise enhanced coordination. Anthropic's Claude 3 shows how improved communication protocols enable better domain interaction through context-aware processing. Meta's CM3leon demonstrates how advanced state management provides more reliable coordination across modalities. NVIDIA's Omniverse reveals how enhanced resource sharing supports efficient operation in virtual environments. These developments may improve system integration while maintaining operational reliability.

Performance optimization continues through various advances. Google's TPU v5 demonstrates how enhanced processing enables more efficient operation in AI workloads. AMD's MI300X shows how improved resource management supports better utilization for complex AI tasks. Intel's Gaudi3 reveals how advanced coordination reduces overhead costs in neural network processing. These improvements may enhance system performance while maintaining reliable function.

Security measures are advancing with emerging requirements. Microsoft's Azure Confidential Computing shows how enhanced protection prevents unauthorized access in sensitive AI workloads. Google Cloud's Security Command Center demonstrates how advanced monitoring identifies potential issues more effectively. Anthropic's constitutional AI reveals how improved response handles ethical considerations better. These developments may strengthen security while maintaining operational efficiency.

Quality assurance is advancing through refined methods. DeepMind's Gemini demonstrates how enhanced testing verifies operation more thoroughly through multimodal validation. OpenAI's evaluation frameworks show how advanced validation confirms reliability better across diverse tasks. Hugging Face's evaluation tools reveal how improved monitoring tracks performance more effectively. These developments may improve quality while maintaining efficiency.

Resource management continues to evolve. AWS Trainium shows how enhanced allocation improves resource distribution for AI training. Azure's AI-optimized infrastructure demonstrates how advanced optimization ensures efficient usage. Google's distributed AI infrastructure reveals how improved monitoring guides resource decisions. These developments may enhance resource utilization while maintaining reliable operation.

Integration frameworks are becoming more sophisticated. PyTorch 2.0 shows how enhanced protocols support better coordination across AI domains. TensorFlow's distributed runtime demonstrates how advanced tools enable easier implementation. JAX reveals how improved management maintains reliable operation across accelerators. These developments may enhance integration while maintaining system reliability.

Documentation systems are evolving to support complexity. GitHub Copilot shows how enhanced technical recording maintains system knowledge through AI assistance. Notion AI demonstrates how advanced operational logging tracks performance better. GitBook's AI features reveal how improved maintenance tracking guides service more effectively. These developments may improve system management while maintaining clarity.

Testing approaches are advancing through new methods. Microsoft's autonomous testing frameworks show how enhanced integration testing verifies coordination better. Google's AI-powered testing tools demonstrate how advanced performance testing confirms reliability more thoroughly. Meta's automated testing infrastructure reveals how improved security testing validates protection better. These developments may enhance testing while maintaining efficiency.

Development tools continue to improve. Amazon CodeWhisperer shows how enhanced creation tools support better implementation through AI assistance. Visual Studio's AI-powered features demonstrate how advanced testing enables thorough validation. GitHub's AI-enhanced tools reveal how improved deployment simplifies distribution. These developments may enhance development while maintaining reliability.

Monitoring capabilities expand through new approaches. Datadog's AI-powered analytics shows how enhanced performance tracking provides better metrics. New Relic's AI operations demonstrate how advanced resource monitoring ensures efficient operation. Dynatrace's AI engine reveals how improved quality tracking verifies reliability better. These developments may improve monitoring while maintaining efficiency.

Error handling is advancing through improved methods. AWS's fault injection simulator shows how enhanced isolation prevents error propagation better. Google's site reliability engineering practices demonstrate how advanced recovery ensures reliable restoration. Azure's chaos engineering tools reveal how improved coordination maintains system integrity. These developments may enhance reliability while maintaining operational efficiency.

Implementation practices continue to mature. MLflow's enhanced features show how improved planning enhances deployment success. Kubeflow demonstrates how advanced integration simplifies connection across AI workflows. Ray's distributed framework reveals how improved management ensures reliable operation. These developments may improve implementation while maintaining standards.

Quality management is advancing through refined approaches. OpenAI's evaluation suite shows how enhanced standards maintain reliable operation better. Google's AI test suites demonstrate how advanced monitoring ensures consistent performance. Microsoft's AI validation frameworks reveal how improved validation confirms reliability better. These developments may enhance quality while maintaining efficiency.

The evolution suggests continuing advancement in several key areas. Anthropic's research into scalable oversight indicates how future AI systems might maintain reliability at scale. DeepMind's work on artificial general intelligence demonstrates potential paths toward more sophisticated multi-domain integration. OpenAI's investigations into multimodal learning suggest new possibilities for cross-domain coordination. These developments may create new opportunities while maintaining essential standards.

Our exploration of cross-domain AI solutions has revealed how multiple artificial intelligence capabilities can work together to create comprehensive solutions while maintaining essential operational standards. From examining fundamental principles of domain integration to investigating practical applications, we've established a comprehensive foundation for implementing these sophisticated combined technologies. Google's Gemini and Anthropic's Claude 3 exemplify this integration, demonstrating how modern AI systems successfully combine language, vision, and reasoning capabilities while maintaining robust performance standards.

The principles we've explored regarding integration frameworks, resource coordination, and multi-domain processing demonstrate how organizations must carefully orchestrate multiple AI capabilities to create effective solutions. Meta's PyTorch ecosystem illustrates these principles in practice, showing how modern development frameworks enable seamless integration of multiple AI domains while maintaining performance and reliability. These lessons prove particularly valuable as we move forward to examine AI Development Challenges, where the complexities of implementation often become most apparent in projects that combine multiple technologies and domains.

The implementation considerations we've examined, from resource requirements and performance optimization to integration needs and quality management, provide valuable context for understanding how organizations deploy sophisticated AI solutions. Microsoft's Azure AI infrastructure demonstrates these considerations in practice, showing how careful attention to system architecture, resource management, and security enables successful deployment of complex AI systems. While specific technologies may differ, the fundamental principles of successful AI implementation persist. This understanding will prove particularly valuable as we examine the common challenges organizations face when developing AI solutions and the strategies for addressing these obstacles effectively.

The relationship between cross-domain projects and development challenges illustrates important parallels in complexity management. Amazon's AWS AI services showcase this relationship, demonstrating how cloud platforms address the challenges of coordinating multiple AI capabilities while maintaining reliability and performance. Where cross-domain projects must coordinate multiple AI capabilities effectively, development challenges often arise from the interactions between different system components and requirements. Understanding these parallels helps organizations prepare for and address common development issues while maintaining project success.

Our journey continues as we examine the challenges organizations face when developing AI solutions and the strategies for overcoming these obstacles. NVIDIA's AI platform illustrates how modern tools and frameworks help organizations address these challenges while maintaining development efficiency. This transition from cross-domain projects to development challenges represents more than a shift in focus, it demonstrates how understanding common implementation difficulties helps organizations create more robust and reliable solutions.

The path ahead reveals how organizations identify, address, and prevent common development challenges while maintaining successful AI implementation. Antrhopic's research into scalable AI systems and OpenAI's work on multimodal learning point toward future developments that will further enhance our ability to create sophisticated cross-domain solutions. This exploration will further expand our understanding of AI's practical implementation possibilities while maintaining focus on creating reliable and effective solutions that stand the test of real-world deployment.

Looking ahead to Chapter 11, we will explore these AI Development Challenges in detail, building upon the cross-domain integration principles we've examined here while focusing on specific strategies for overcoming common obstacles in AI implementation. The foundations we've established in understanding cross-domain integration will prove invaluable as we investigate how organizations can successfully navigate the complexities of AI development while maintaining robust and reliable solutions.

CHAPTER 11: AI DEVELOPMENT CHALLENGES

Our exploration of artificial intelligence now turns to the critical examination of development challenges that shape implementation success. Having explored various AI domains and their integration, we now investigate the common obstacles organizations face when developing AI solutions and the strategies for addressing these challenges effectively.

The journey of AI development often encounters significant hurdles that must be carefully navigated. From ensuring data quality and maintaining model performance to managing computational resources and addressing implementation complexities, these challenges represent crucial aspects of AI development that demand systematic approaches and careful consideration.

Understanding development challenges proves particularly significant in light of our previous explorations. While individual AI domains present their specific difficulties, certain fundamental challenges persist across all implementations. Data quality affects language processing just as it impacts computer vision. Resource constraints influence gaming AI as

245

much as robotics applications. Integration challenges appear in cross-domain projects and single-domain implementations alike.

The relationship between development challenges and successful implementation demonstrates the crucial importance of understanding and preparing for common obstacles. Organizations that anticipate and plan for these challenges often achieve more reliable implementations. Those that develop systematic approaches to addressing these issues typically create more sustainable solutions.

As we begin our examination of AI development challenges, we'll explore how organizations identify, address, and overcome common obstacles while maintaining implementation effectiveness. From understanding fundamental issues in data quality and model performance to examining specific approaches for resource management and implementation challenges, our journey reveals how organizations create successful solutions despite common development hurdles.

The path ahead illuminates the strategies and methods organizations employ to address development challenges while maintaining successful AI implementation. Understanding these challenges and their solutions helps create more reliable and effective AI solutions that can withstand the rigors of practical deployment.

Data quality challenges represent fundamental obstacles in AI development that significantly influence solution effectiveness. Understanding and addressing these challenges proves essential for creating reliable AI implementations.

Data availability presents significant challenges in AI development. Sufficient quantities of relevant data may not exist for specific applications. Available data might not represent all necessary scenarios or conditions. Legal or privacy restrictions may limit data access. These availability issues significantly affect development capabilities.

Quality assessment requires systematic approaches. Data

validation verifies accuracy and completeness. Consistency checking identifies discrepancies and anomalies. Format verification ensures appropriate structure. Statistical analysis reveals potential quality issues. These assessment methods help maintain data reliability.

Data cleansing addresses quality issues. Missing value handling requires appropriate strategies. Outlier detection identifies anomalous data. Error correction fixes identified issues. Standardization ensures consistent formats. These cleansing processes help maintain data quality.

Data augmentation provides solutions for limited datasets. Image transformation creates additional training examples. Text variation generates alternative expressions. Sound modification produces audio variations. These augmentation approaches help address data limitations while maintaining relevance.

Synthetic data generation offers additional solutions. Statistical modeling creates realistic synthetic examples. Generative models produce artificial data. Simulation systems generate scenario-based information. These generation approaches help supplement available data while maintaining quality standards.

Validation techniques verify data suitability. Cross-validation confirms representativeness. Distribution analysis verifies statistical properties. Domain validation ensures relevance. These validation approaches help maintain data reliability.

Quality management implements ongoing monitoring. Regular assessment tracks data quality. Issue identification enables prompt resolution. Quality metrics guide improvement efforts. These management practices help maintain data effectiveness.

Bias detection requires careful attention. Statistical analysis identifies potential bias. Representation checking verifies coverage. Impact assessment evaluates consequences. These detection approaches help maintain fair data usage.

Documentation requirements support quality management. Data sources require clear documentation. Processing steps need detailed records. Quality measures demand careful tracking. These documentation practices help maintain data understanding.

Version control manages data evolution. Dataset versions track changes over time. Processing history maintains modification records. Distribution management enables controlled access. These control measures help maintain data consistency.

Storage management ensures data availability. Appropriate infrastructure supports data volume. Access methods enable efficient retrieval. Backup systems prevent data loss. These management practices help maintain data accessibility.

Privacy protection implements necessary safeguards. Anonymization removes identifying information. Access control restricts data usage. Security measures protect sensitive information. These protection measures help maintain appropriate privacy.

Quality metrics track data characteristics. Completeness measures verify full coverage. Accuracy metrics assess correctness. Consistency measures track reliable representation. These metrics help maintain quality awareness.

Update procedures maintain current data. Regular updates incorporate new information. Quality verification confirms continued reliability. Distribution ensures appropriate access. These procedures help maintain data currency.

Integration requirements affect quality management. Format compatibility ensures smooth integration. Quality standards maintain consistent requirements. Validation processes verify successful combination. These requirements help maintain effective integration.

Resource implications influence quality management. Storage requirements affect infrastructure needs. Processing demands influence computational resources. Management overhead requires appropriate staffing. These implications help guide resource planning.

Cost considerations affect quality approaches. Data acquisition involves various expenses. Quality management requires ongoing investment. Infrastructure needs demand appropriate funding. These considerations help guide quality decisions.

Future planning addresses ongoing needs. Data volume continues growing. Quality requirements evolve over time. Management needs change with scale. These planning considerations help maintain sustainable approaches.

Model performance challenges represent critical obstacles in AI development that significantly affect solution effectiveness. Understanding and addressing these challenges proves essential for creating reliable AI implementations.

Overfitting prevention remains a fundamental challenge. Models may learn training data patterns too precisely, limiting generalization to new situations. Cross-validation helps identify overfitting early. Regularization techniques provide systematic prevention. Early stopping prevents excessive training. These prevention approaches help maintain model reliability.

Regularization methods implement specific controls. L1 regularization encourages sparse feature usage. L2 regularization prevents excessive weight values. Dropout techniques reduce dependency on specific neurons. These regularization approaches help maintain appropriate model complexity.

Cross-validation approaches verify model performance. K-fold validation tests different data splits. Hold-out validation reserves testing data. Time-series validation respects temporal order. These validation approaches help confirm reliable operation.

Performance optimization addresses various aspects. Learning rate adjustment affects training speed. Batch size selection influences learning stability. Architecture optimization improves processing efficiency. These optimization approaches help maintain effective operation.

Model selection criteria guide implementation choices. Complexity requirements influence architecture decisions. Resource constraints affect model options. Performance needs guide capability choices. These selection criteria help create appropriate solutions.

Evaluation methods verify model effectiveness. Accuracy metrics measure prediction quality. Performance metrics track processing efficiency. Resource metrics monitor utilization levels. These evaluation approaches help maintain reliable assessment.

Training challenges require specific attention. Learning stability needs careful monitoring. Convergence issues demand appropriate response. Resource usage requires efficient management. These training considerations help maintain effective development.

Architecture optimization influences performance. Layer configuration affects processing capability. Node connections impact learning capacity. Activation functions influence model behavior. These optimization approaches help create efficient solutions.

Resource utilization affects model performance. Memory usage demands careful management. Processing requirements need efficient allocation. Network utilization requires appropriate optimization. These utilization considerations help maintain efficient operation.

Error analysis guides performance improvement. Pattern identification reveals systematic issues. Root cause analysis identifies underlying problems. Solution development addresses identified issues. These analysis approaches help maintain continuous improvement.

Validation requirements ensure reliable operation. Test data verifies general performance. Validation data confirms learning effectiveness. Production data validates real-world operation. These validation approaches help maintain reliable solutions.

Performance monitoring tracks operational status. Response time measurement verifies timeliness. Accuracy tracking confirms reliable operation. Resource monitoring ensures efficient usage. These monitoring approaches help maintain effective operation.

Documentation needs support performance management. Architecture documentation describes model structure. Training documentation records development process. Performance documentation tracks operational characteristics. These documentation practices help maintain solution knowledge.

Version control manages model evolution. Change tracking maintains modification history. Performance comparison enables progress assessment. Rollback capability ensures reliable recovery. These control measures help maintain solution reliability.

Quality assurance implements systematic verification. Performance testing confirms reliable operation. Integration testing verifies system coordination. Security testing validates protection measures. These assurance approaches help maintain solution quality.

Maintenance requirements ensure ongoing effectiveness. Regular updates maintain current capabilities. Performance optimization improves efficiency. Issue resolution addresses operational problems. These maintenance practices help maintain reliable operation.

Cost implications influence performance decisions. Development expenses affect implementation choices. Operational costs impact ongoing management. Optimization needs require appropriate investment. These cost considerations help guide performance planning.

Future planning addresses ongoing development. Performance requirements continue evolving. Resource needs change over time. Capability demands grow with usage. These planning considerations help maintain sustainable solutions.

Resource management challenges represent significant

obstacles in AI development that affect implementation success. Understanding and addressing these challenges proves essential for maintaining effective operations while controlling costs.

Computational requirements present fundamental challenges. Processing needs vary significantly between models. Memory demands grow with data volume. Storage requirements increase with solution complexity. GPU resources affect training capabilities. These requirements significantly influence implementation possibilities.

Hardware limitations affect development options. Processing capacity constrains model complexity. Memory limits affect data handling capability. Storage capacity influences dataset size. Network bandwidth impacts distributed operation. These limitations shape implementation approaches.

Resource optimization requires systematic approaches. Processing distribution balances computational load. Memory management ensures efficient usage. Storage optimization maintains appropriate capacity. Network utilization requires careful management. These optimization approaches help maintain efficient operation.

Scaling considerations affect resource planning. User growth increases processing demands. Data volume expansion affects storage needs. Feature addition impacts resource requirements. Geographic distribution influences network needs. These scaling factors help guide resource allocation.

Cost management implements budget controls. Hardware expenses require careful planning. Software licensing needs appropriate budgeting. Support costs demand ongoing funding. Operational expenses need systematic management. These management practices help maintain sustainable operation.

Efficiency improvements address resource usage. Algorithm optimization reduces processing needs. Data structure optimization improves memory usage. Storage optimization enhances capacity utilization. These improvements help maintain efficient operation.

Infrastructure planning supports resource needs. Hardware selection matches processing requirements. Network configuration enables appropriate communication. Storage systems provide necessary capacity. Power systems ensure reliable operation. These planning approaches help create effective environments.

Capacity planning addresses future needs. Growth projections guide resource allocation. Usage patterns influence planning decisions. Technology evolution affects future requirements. These planning considerations help maintain adequate resources.

Monitoring systems track resource usage. Performance monitoring measures processing efficiency. Memory tracking verifies efficient usage. Storage monitoring ensures appropriate capacity. Network monitoring confirms reliable operation. These monitoring practices help maintain effective management.

Resource allocation implements systematic distribution. Processing assignment matches computational needs. Memory allocation ensures efficient usage. Storage assignment provides appropriate capacity. These allocation practices help maintain efficient operation.

Maintenance requirements ensure ongoing reliability. Regular updates maintain current capabilities. Performance optimization improves efficiency. Issue resolution addresses operational problems. These maintenance practices help maintain reliable operation.

Documentation needs support resource management. Infrastructure documentation describes system configuration. Usage documentation tracks resource utilization. Planning documentation guides future development. These documentation practices help maintain system knowledge.

Cost analysis guides resource decisions. Hardware costs influence implementation choices. Software expenses affect solution options. Operational costs impact ongoing management. These cost considerations help guide resource planning.

Quality assurance verifies resource usage. Performance testing confirms efficient operation. Capacity testing verifies adequate resources. Stress testing validates system limits. These assurance practices help maintain reliable operation.

Security implementation protects resources. Access control manages system usage. Monitoring systems track unusual activity. Protection measures prevent unauthorized use. These security practices help maintain safe operation.

Disaster recovery ensures operational continuity. Backup systems protect essential data. Recovery procedures restore operation. Testing validates recovery capability. These recovery practices help maintain reliable operation.

Version management maintains system currency. Update procedures keep systems current. Testing processes verify changes. Rollback capabilities ensure reliability. These management practices help maintain effective operation.

Future planning addresses ongoing needs. Resource requirements continue evolving. Technology options change over time. Cost structures shift with market conditions. These planning considerations help maintain sustainable solutions.

Implementation challenges represent complex obstacles that organizations face when deploying AI solutions. Understanding and addressing these challenges proves essential for successful deployment and ongoing operation.

Integration issues affect system coordination. Component compatibility requires careful verification. Interface design needs appropriate standardization. Data flow demands efficient management. Communication protocols need reliable implementation. System coordination requires effective orchestration. These integration considerations significantly influence implementation success.

Performance bottlenecks limit system effectiveness. Processing delays affect response time. Memory constraints impact operation speed. Network limitations restrict data flow. Storage access slows system operation. Resource contention reduces efficiency. Cache management affects performance. These bottlenecks require systematic identification and resolution.

Deployment problems affect system availability. Configuration management needs careful attention. Environment setup requires appropriate preparation. Version control demands systematic management. Distribution systems need reliable operation. Installation procedures require clear documentation. Update processes need careful coordination. These deployment issues influence operational success.

Version management challenges affect system stability. Update coordination requires careful planning. Compatibility verification needs systematic testing. Rollback capabilities demand reliable implementation. Distribution management requires efficient processes. Version tracking needs accurate records. Change management demands clear procedures. These management challenges affect operational reliability.

System coordination issues impact effectiveness. Component interaction needs careful design. Resource sharing requires efficient management. State synchronization demands reliable mechanisms. Error handling needs systematic approaches. Recovery procedures require clear definition. Operation monitoring needs continuous attention. These coordination issues influence system reliability.

Maintenance difficulties affect ongoing operation. Update procedures require careful planning. Performance optimization needs systematic approach. Issue resolution demands efficient processes. Documentation maintenance requires ongoing attention. Support procedures need clear definition. Resource management demands careful attention. These maintenance challenges impact operational success.

Testing requirements ensure reliable operation. Unit testing verifies component function. Integration testing confirms system coordination. Performance testing validates operational efficiency. Security testing ensures appropriate protection. User testing verifies practical utility. Regression testing maintains reliability. These testing needs affect implementation quality.

Documentation challenges impact system understanding. Technical documentation requires clear explanation. User documentation needs appropriate detail. Operation documentation demands regular updates. Maintenance documentation requires systematic management. Version documentation needs accurate records. Process documentation demands clear procedures. These documentation issues affect system maintainability.

Security implementation presents specific challenges. Access control requires careful management. Data protection needs appropriate measures. Operation monitoring demands continuous attention. Incident response requires clear procedures. Compliance verification needs systematic approach. Risk management demands ongoing attention. These security challenges affect system safety.

Quality assurance demands systematic approaches. Performance standards require clear definition. Testing procedures need systematic implementation. Validation processes demand careful execution. Documentation requirements need appropriate attention. Review procedures require regular execution. Improvement processes demand continuous focus. These quality considerations affect implementation success.

Resource management challenges affect operation. Processing allocation requires efficient distribution. Memory management needs careful optimization. Storage utilization demands appropriate planning. Network usage requires efficient management. Power consumption needs careful consideration. Cost control demands ongoing attention. These management issues influence operational efficiency.

Time management affects implementation progress.

Schedule planning requires realistic assessment. Resource allocation needs appropriate coordination. Milestone tracking demands regular attention. Progress monitoring requires continuous focus. Issue resolution needs timely response. Risk management demands proactive approach. These time factors impact implementation success.

Team coordination challenges affect development. Communication needs effective channels. Responsibility assignment requires clear definition. Progress tracking demands regular updates. Issue resolution needs systematic approach. Knowledge sharing requires efficient methods. Skill development demands ongoing attention. These coordination issues influence implementation effectiveness.

Change management presents specific challenges. Process modification requires careful planning. User adaptation needs appropriate support. System transition demands systematic approach. Impact assessment requires thorough analysis. Risk management needs careful attention. Communication demands clear procedures. These management issues affect implementation acceptance.

Performance optimization challenges affect operation. Processing efficiency requires systematic improvement. Memory utilization needs careful management. Network optimization demands appropriate attention. Storage access requires efficient methods. Resource usage needs continuous monitoring. Cost effectiveness demands ongoing focus. These optimization issues influence operational efficiency.

Future planning addresses ongoing development. Capability requirements continue evolving. Technology options change over time. Resource needs shift with growth. Cost structures require regular review. Support needs demand ongoing assessment. These planning considerations help maintain sustainable solutions.

Quality management ensures reliable operation. Performance monitoring tracks system behavior. Issue identification enables prompt resolution. Improvement implementation maintains effectiveness. Documentation updates preserve knowledge. Training maintains operational capability. These management practices help maintain reliable solutions.

Integration planning guides implementation success. Component selection ensures compatibility. Resource allocation maintains efficiency. Timeline management coordinates development. Quality assurance verifies reliability. These planning considerations help create effective solutions.

Challenge resolution methods provide systematic approaches for addressing AI development obstacles. Understanding these methods proves essential for maintaining effective development progress and ensuring successful implementation.

Problem identification implements systematic analysis. Issue tracking maintains comprehensive records. Impact assessment evaluates effect severity. Root cause analysis identifies underlying factors. Pattern recognition reveals systematic issues. Priority assessment guides response order. Resource evaluation determines resolution needs. These identification approaches help target effective solutions.

Solution development follows structured approaches. Option analysis evaluates possible responses. Resource assessment determines implementation feasibility. Timeline planning establishes resolution schedule. Cost evaluation determines resource requirements. Risk assessment identifies potential issues. Implementation planning guides solution deployment. These development practices help create effective responses.

Testing approaches verify solution effectiveness. Component testing validates specific fixes. Integration testing confirms system coordination. Performance testing verifies operational improvement. Security testing ensures maintained protection. User testing validates practical utility. Regression testing confirms maintained functionality. These testing methods help ensure reliable solutions.

Validation methods confirm resolution success. Performance verification ensures improved operation. Integration validation confirms system coordination. Security validation verifies maintained protection. User validation confirms practical effectiveness. Documentation validation ensures accurate records. Resource validation confirms efficient usage. These validation approaches help maintain solution quality.

Implementation strategies guide solution deployment. Rollout planning ensures systematic deployment. Resource allocation supports implementation needs. Timeline management coordinates deployment steps. Risk management addresses potential issues. Communication planning ensures stakeholder awareness. Training preparation supports effective adoption. These strategies help ensure successful deployment.

Success measurement tracks resolution effectiveness. Performance metrics verify improvement levels. Resource metrics confirm efficient usage. User metrics validate practical utility. Cost metrics evaluate resource efficiency. Time metrics track implementation speed. Quality metrics ensure maintained standards. These measurements help verify solution effectiveness.

Quality assurance implements systematic verification. Testing procedures confirm resolution effectiveness. Documentation updates maintain accurate records. Performance monitoring tracks ongoing operation. Security verification ensures maintained protection. Integration validation confirms system coordination. These assurance practices help maintain solution reliability.

Resource management supports resolution efforts. Processing allocation ensures computational availability. Memory management maintains efficient usage. Storage allocation provides necessary capacity. Network resources support distributed operation. These management practices help maintain efficient resolution.

Documentation requirements maintain solution knowledge. Resolution records track implementation details. Performance documentation verifies improvement levels. Configuration documentation maintains system information. Process documentation guides future efforts. These documentation practices help preserve solution understanding.

Training needs support effective implementation. User training ensures proper solution usage. Technical training supports implementation capability. Support training enables effective assistance. Documentation training maintains knowledge access. These training practices help maintain solution effectiveness.

Communication planning ensures stakeholder awareness. Status updates maintain progress information. Issue notification enables prompt response. Resolution communication provides success confirmation. Documentation updates maintain current knowledge. These communication practices help maintain effective coordination.

Cost management guides resource allocation. Development expenses require appropriate budgeting. Implementation costs need careful planning. Operation expenses demand ongoing management. Support costs require sustained funding. These management practices help maintain sustainable solutions.

Time management coordinates resolution efforts. Schedule planning ensures realistic timelines. Resource allocation supports efficient progress. Milestone tracking maintains implementation focus. Progress monitoring enables timely adjustment. These management practices help maintain effective progress.

Quality management ensures maintained standards. Performance monitoring tracks operational reliability. Issue identification enables prompt response. Resolution verification confirms effectiveness. Documentation updates preserve knowledge. These management practices help maintain solution quality.

Future planning addresses ongoing needs. Resolution requirements continue evolving. Technology options change over time. Resource needs shift with growth. Support demands require regular assessment. These planning considerations help maintain sustainable solutions.

Integration requirements affect resolution approaches. Component compatibility needs careful verification. Interface design requires appropriate standardization. Data flow demands efficient management. System coordination requires effective orchestration. These requirements help guide effective solutions.

Security considerations influence resolution methods. Access control maintains appropriate protection. Data security ensures information safety. Operation monitoring tracks system activity. Incident response enables prompt action. These considerations help maintain secure solutions.

Documentation maintenance supports ongoing operation. Technical records maintain solution details. Process documentation guides implementation steps. Configuration records track system settings. These maintenance practices help preserve solution knowledge.

Development best practices provide proven approaches for creating reliable AI solutions while avoiding common pitfalls. Understanding and implementing these practices proves essential for maintaining development effectiveness and ensuring implementation success.

Quality standards establish fundamental requirements. Code quality demands systematic review. Documentation quality requires clear standards. Testing quality needs comprehensive coverage. Performance quality establishes operational targets. Security quality demands appropriate protection. Integration quality requires reliable coordination. These standards help maintain reliable development.

Testing protocols implement systematic verification. Unit

testing validates component function. Integration testing confirms system coordination. Performance testing verifies operational efficiency. Security testing ensures appropriate protection. User testing validates practical utility. Regression testing maintains existing functionality. These protocols help ensure reliable operation.

Documentation requirements maintain system knowledge. Architecture documentation describes system structure. Code documentation explains implementation details. API documentation guides interface usage. Operation documentation supports system management. User documentation enables effective usage. Maintenance documentation guides ongoing support. These requirements help preserve solution understanding.

Management approaches guide development efforts. Project planning establishes clear objectives. Resource allocation ensures appropriate support. Timeline management coordinates development activities. Risk management addresses potential issues. Quality management maintains reliable operation. Change management guides system evolution. These approaches help maintain effective development.

Version control implements systematic management. Code versioning tracks implementation changes. Documentation versioning maintains current records. Configuration versioning preserves system settings. Release management coordinates updates. Distribution management enables controlled access. These practices help maintain reliable development.

Review processes verify development quality. Code reviews examine implementation details. Design reviews validate system architecture. Documentation reviews verify information accuracy. Performance reviews assess operational efficiency. Security reviews confirm protection measures. These processes help maintain solution quality.

Integration practices ensure reliable coordination.

Component integration validates compatibility. System integration confirms coordination. Performance integration verifies efficient operation. Security integration ensures maintained protection. These practices help create reliable solutions.

Testing strategies guide verification efforts. Test planning establishes coverage requirements. Resource allocation supports testing needs. Automation implementation improves efficiency. Result analysis guides improvement efforts. Documentation maintains testing knowledge. These strategies help ensure thorough verification.

Security implementation maintains appropriate protection. Access control manages system usage. Data protection ensures information safety. Operation monitoring tracks system activity. Incident response enables prompt action. Compliance verification confirms requirement adherence. These implementations help maintain secure operation.

Performance optimization improves operational efficiency. Code optimization enhances processing speed. Resource optimization ensures efficient usage. Integration optimization improves coordination. Documentation optimization maintains clear records. These optimizations help maintain efficient operation.

Quality assurance implements systematic verification. Process validation confirms proper execution. Result validation verifies accurate output. Documentation validation ensures clear records. Integration validation confirms proper coordination. These assurance practices help maintain reliable solutions.

Maintenance procedures support ongoing operation. Update management maintains current capabilities. Issue resolution addresses operational problems. Performance optimization improves efficiency. Documentation updates preserve knowledge. These procedures help maintain reliable operation.

Development environments support efficient creation.

Tool selection provides appropriate capabilities. Configuration management maintains consistent settings. Integration support enables effective coordination. Documentation access preserves knowledge availability. These environments help maintain productive development.

Team coordination ensures effective collaboration. Communication channels maintain information flow. Responsibility assignment clarifies ownership. Progress tracking monitors development status. Issue management enables prompt resolution. These coordination practices help maintain efficient development.

Resource management optimizes development support. Processing allocation ensures computational availability. Storage management maintains efficient usage. Network resources support distributed operation. Tool licensing manages software access. These management practices help maintain efficient development.

Documentation maintenance preserves system knowledge. Technical documentation maintains implementation details. Process documentation guides operational procedures. Configuration documentation preserves system settings. User documentation supports effective usage. These maintenance practices help preserve solution understanding.

Quality management ensures reliable development. Performance monitoring tracks operational efficiency. Issue identification enables prompt response. Resolution implementation maintains effectiveness. Documentation updates preserve knowledge. These management practices help maintain reliable solutions.

Continuous improvement supports ongoing enhancement. Process analysis identifies improvement opportunities. Implementation planning guides enhancement efforts. Result validation confirms improvement effectiveness. Documentation updates maintain current knowledge. These improvement practices help maintain development effectiveness.

The future of AI development challenges continues to evolve as technology advances and implementation experience grows. Understanding emerging trends and potential developments helps organizations prepare for future obstacles while maintaining effective development practices.

Challenge evolution suggests continuing advancement. Data quality issues become more complex with increasing volume. Performance requirements grow more demanding with expanded applications. Resource needs increase with solution sophistication. Integration challenges expand with system complexity. These evolutionary patterns help guide preparation efforts.

Solution approaches continue developing. Automated testing enhances verification capabilities. Improved monitoring provides better operational insight. Advanced optimization enables more efficient operation. Enhanced integration simplifies system coordination. These developments may improve challenge resolution while maintaining reliability.

Tool capabilities expand through ongoing advancement. Development environments provide enhanced support. Testing frameworks enable more thorough verification. Monitoring systems offer improved insight. Management tools provide better control. These capabilities may enhance development effectiveness while maintaining quality standards.

Resource management is advancing through new approaches. Enhanced allocation improves resource distribution. Advanced optimization ensures efficient usage. Improved monitoring guides resource decisions. Automated management reduces manual effort. These developments may enhance resource utilization while maintaining operational efficiency.

Quality assurance is advancing through refined methods. Enhanced testing verifies operation more thoroughly. Advanced validation confirms reliability better. Improved monitoring tracks performance more effectively. Automated verification reduces manual effort. These developments may improve quality while maintaining efficiency.

Documentation systems are evolving to support complexity. Enhanced technical recording maintains system knowledge. Advanced operational logging tracks performance better. Improved maintenance tracking guides service more effectively. Automated generation reduces manual effort. These developments may improve system management while maintaining clarity.

Security measures are advancing with emerging threats. Enhanced protection prevents unauthorized access. Advanced monitoring identifies potential issues more effectively. Improved response handles security incidents better. Automated defense reduces manual intervention. These developments may strengthen security while maintaining operational efficiency.

Integration capabilities expand through standardization efforts. Enhanced protocols enable better system connection. Improved data exchange supports comprehensive operation. Standardized interfaces simplify implementation. Automated integration reduces manual effort. These advances may improve system integration while maintaining reliability.

Performance optimization continues through various approaches. Enhanced processing improves operational efficiency. Advanced resource usage optimizes system operation. Improved monitoring guides optimization efforts. Automated optimization reduces manual tuning. These developments may improve performance while maintaining reliability.

Development practices continue to mature. Enhanced planning improves implementation success. Advanced integration simplifies connection. Improved management ensures reliable operation. Automated processes reduce manual effort. These developments may improve implementation while maintaining standards.

Team coordination is advancing through new methods. Enhanced communication improves information sharing. Advanced tracking provides better progress insight. Improved collaboration enables effective teamwork. Automated coordination reduces manual effort. These developments may enhance team effectiveness while maintaining efficiency.

Cost management is improving through enhanced analysis. Better resource allocation optimizes expenses. Improved efficiency reduces operational costs. Advanced planning guides investment decisions. Automated management reduces manual effort. These developments may improve cost effectiveness while maintaining capability.

Quality management is advancing through refined approaches. Enhanced standards maintain reliable operation better. Advanced monitoring ensures consistent performance. Improved validation confirms reliability better. Automated verification reduces manual effort. These developments may enhance quality while maintaining efficiency.

Documentation approaches are evolving to meet changing needs. Enhanced systems provide better knowledge capture. Advanced organization improves information access. Improved maintenance ensures current content. Automated generation reduces manual effort. These developments may enhance documentation while maintaining clarity.

Testing approaches are advancing through new methods. Enhanced frameworks provide better coverage. Advanced automation improves efficiency. Improved analysis guides testing efforts. Automated verification reduces manual effort. These developments may improve testing while maintaining thoroughness.

Future possibilities are emerging through ongoing research. New capabilities advance through careful validation. Implementation options expand with experience. Automation opportunities increase with technology. These developments may create new opportunities while maintaining essential standards.

Challenge resolution methods continue to evolve. Enhanced identification improves problem detection. Advanced analysis guides solution development. Improved implementation ensures effective resolution. Automated handling reduces manual effort. These developments may improve resolution while maintaining reliability.

The evolution suggests continuing advancement in capabilities, implementation approaches, and operational practices. Organizations must maintain awareness of these developments while planning current implementations to ensure sustainable, effective solutions.

Our exploration of AI development challenges completes our journey through the practical implementation of artificial intelligence solutions. From examining fundamental obstacles in data quality and model performance to investigating resource management and implementation challenges, we've established a comprehensive understanding of the difficulties organizations face and the methods for addressing them effectively.

The principles we've explored regarding challenge identification, resolution methods, and best practices demonstrate how organizations can systematically approach and overcome development obstacles. This understanding proves particularly valuable as organizations implement the various AI capabilities we've examined throughout this book, from language processing and data analysis to gaming systems and cross-domain integration.

Throughout our journey, we've progressed from understanding AI fundamentals in Book One to exploring practical implementation in this volume. We've examined how organizations leverage various AI capabilities, implement different types of solutions, and address the challenges that arise during development. This progression provides a comprehensive foundation for working with artificial intelligence technology effectively.

The relationship between development challenges and

successful implementation illuminates crucial aspects of AI development. Whether implementing language processing systems, developing computer vision solutions, or creating cross-domain applications, organizations must anticipate and address common challenges while maintaining development effectiveness. Understanding these challenges and their solutions helps create more reliable and sustainable implementations.

As we conclude both this chapter and Book Two of the *NewBits AI Trilogy*, we set the stage for exploring cutting-edge developments in Book Three, *AI Frontier: Navigating the Cutting Edge*. The understanding we've developed of implementation challenges and their solutions will prove particularly valuable as we examine emerging technologies and new possibilities in artificial intelligence.

The journey continues as we move forward to explore the frontiers of AI technology, building upon our understanding of both fundamental principles and practical implementation. This foundation in addressing development challenges will help guide our exploration of new capabilities while maintaining focus on creating reliable and effective solutions.

PREVIEW OF BOOK THREE, *AI FRONTIER: NAVIGATING THE CUTTING EDGE*

Having established both fundamental understanding and practical implementation knowledge, our journey advances to explore current breakthroughs and future directions in artificial intelligence. The final book in the *NewBits AI Trilogy* examines verified advances while thoughtfully considering future possibilities.

AI Frontier: Navigating the Cutting Edge begins with an examination of core technological breakthroughs. We explore documented advances in machine learning architectures, neural network designs, and natural language processing capabilities. These fundamental developments provide context for understanding how AI technology continues to evolve while maintaining connection to established principles.

The journey then returns to our six key categories of AI solutions, examining cutting-edge developments in each domain. We investigate recent breakthroughs in language AI that enhance communication capabilities, advances in data AI that improve analytical power, and innovations in

271

audio/vision AI that expand perceptual abilities. We explore verified developments in healthcare AI that enhance medical capabilities, examine proven advances in robotics AI that enable new forms of automation, and investigate documented progress in gaming AI that creates more sophisticated experiences.

Looking toward tomorrow, we thoughtfully consider future directions grounded in current capabilities and research. This forward-looking perspective examines potential developments while maintaining clear distinction between verified advances and anticipated possibilities. This balanced approach helps prepare you for continued evolution in AI technology while maintaining practical focus.

Throughout *AI Frontier*, we maintain our commitment to factual accuracy while engaging with the excitement of technological advancement. Each chapter builds your understanding of current developments while thoughtfully considering future directions. This exploration builds naturally from the practical implementation knowledge established in this second book while preparing you for the continued evolution of artificial intelligence.

I look forward to seeing you in Book Three as we explore both verified advances and future possibilities in artificial intelligence technology.

AI GLOSSARY: BIT BY BIT

Welcome to the AI Glossary: Bit By Bit. This glossary breaks down essential AI and machine learning terms, from basic data units to advanced concepts. Whether you're new to AI or an expert, the following definitions are provided to illuminate your journey into the world of artificial intelligence.

A

A/B Testing - A method to compare two versions of a model or algorithm by testing them on separate datasets to identify the more effective one.

AI Alignment - Ensuring that AI systems' goals and behaviors align with human values and objectives.

AI Ethics - The study of ethical issues in the design, development, and deployment of AI systems.

AI Model - A mathematical or computational structure that an AI system uses to solve problems or make predictions.

AI Platform - Software that provides tools and environments for developing, training, and deploying AI models.

273

AI Safety - Research aimed at ensuring that AI systems operate safely and without unintended consequences.

AI System - A combination of hardware and software components used to perform tasks typically requiring human intelligence.

AI Tool - Software or utility that supports AI development, testing, or deployment.

Activation Function - A function used in neural networks to introduce non-linearity, enabling the model to learn from complex patterns.

Active Learning - A machine learning method where the model selectively queries the most informative data points for labeling.

Actor-Critic Model (Reinforcement Learning) - A framework in reinforcement learning where the 'actor' updates policies, and the 'critic' evaluates the action.

Adversarial Attack - A type of attack where inputs are modified to fool AI models into making incorrect predictions.

Adversarial Example - Data that has been intentionally perturbed to cause an AI system to make mistakes.

Algorithm - A set of rules or processes followed in problem-solving or computation, used by AI systems to make decisions.

Anomaly Detection - Identifying patterns or data points that deviate significantly from the norm.

Artificial General Intelligence (AGI) - A form of AI with the ability to understand, learn, and apply intelligence across a broad range of tasks, similar to human intelligence.

Artificial Intelligence (AI) - The simulation of human intelligence by machines, particularly in problem-solving, learning, and decision-making.

Artificial Neural Network (ANN) - A computational model inspired by the way biological neural networks in the human brain process information.

Attention Head (Deep Learning, Transformers) - A component in transformer models that processes input data to focus on relevant aspects for making predictions.

Attention Mechanism - A technique that enables models to focus on specific parts of the input data when making decisions.

Augmented Reality (AR) - An interactive experience where real-world environments are enhanced by computer-generated perceptual information.

Automated Machine Learning (AutoML) - The process of automating the end-to-end process of applying machine learning to real-world problems.

Autonomous - Refers to systems or vehicles capable of making decisions and operating independently without human intervention.

Autonomous Vehicle - A vehicle capable of sensing its environment and navigating without human input, typically using AI systems.

B

BCI (Brain-Computer Interface) - a technology that enables direct communication between the brain and external devices, often using AI to interpret brain signals.

Backpropagation - An algorithm used to calculate gradients in neural networks during the training phase to minimize the error.

Backward Chaining - A reasoning method that starts with a goal and works backward to determine the necessary conditions to achieve that goal.

Batch Normalization (Deep Learning) - A technique that normalizes inputs in a neural network to speed up training and improve performance.

Bayesian Network - A graphical model representing probabilistic relationships among a set of variables.

Bias - Systematic error in AI models, often caused by unbalanced datasets or faulty assumptions.

Bias-Variance Tradeoff (Machine Learning) - The tradeoff between the error introduced by the bias of the model and the variance in the model's predictions.

Big Data - Large datasets that are complex and require advanced methods for processing and analysis.

Biometric AI - AI systems that analyze and interpret biological data, such as fingerprints, facial recognition, or voice recognition.

Bit - The smallest unit of data in computing, represented as 0 or 1.

Bounding Box - A rectangular box used in computer vision to define the location of an object in an image or video.

Byte - A data unit typically consisting of 8 bits, representing a character in computing.

C

C - A general-purpose, procedural computer programming language supporting structured programming.

C# - A modern, object-oriented programming language developed by Microsoft as part of its .NET framework.

C++ - An extension of the C programming language that adds object-oriented features.

CSS (Cascading Style Sheets) - A style sheet language used for describing the presentation of a document written in HTML or XML.

Capsule Network (ANN, Deep Learning) - A type of neural network designed to handle complex hierarchical relationships more effectively than traditional convolutional networks.

Central Processing Unit (CPU) - The primary component of a computer responsible for executing instructions from programs. In AI, the CPU handles general-purpose processing tasks and is used in training and running machine learning models, though it is typically slower for parallel tasks compared to GPUs or TPUs.

Chatbot - A program that uses AI to simulate conversations with users, often used in customer service or personal assistants.

Classification - The process of categorizing data into predefined classes.

Clustering - A technique used to group similar data points together based on certain features.

Cognitive Computing - AI systems that aim to mimic human cognitive functions such as reasoning and learning.

Computer Vision - A field of AI that enables machines to interpret and make decisions based on visual data.

Computer-Generated Imagery (CGI) - The use of AI and other technologies to create images and animations for media and entertainment.

Convergence (Optimization in ML) - The point during optimization when the model parameters stop changing significantly and the learning process stabilizes.

Convolutional Neural Network (CNN) - A deep learning algorithm commonly used in image recognition and processing tasks.

Cross-Entropy Loss (Loss Function) - A loss function commonly used in classification tasks, measuring the difference between predicted probabilities and actual labels.

Cross-validation - A technique for assessing how a machine learning model will generalize to an independent dataset by partitioning the data into training and testing sets.

Crowdsourcing (Data Collection) - The practice of outsourcing tasks, such as data labeling, to a large group of people or the public.

D

Data Augmentation - A technique to increase the diversity of a training dataset by applying random transformations to the data.

Data Drift - Changes in data distributions over time that can negatively affect model performance.

Data Governance - The set of policies and procedures that manage the availability, integrity, security, and usability of data in an organization. In AI, strong data governance ensures that data used for training and decision-making is reliable, secure, and compliant with relevant laws and standards.

Data Labeling - The process of assigning meaningful labels to raw data for training machine learning models.

Data Mining - The process of discovering patterns and insights from large datasets.

Data Preprocessing - The stage where data is cleaned and transformed before being used to train machine learning models.

Decision Boundary - A surface that separates different classes in a classification problem.

Decision Tree - A supervised learning algorithm used for both classification and regression tasks by splitting data into branches.

Deep Learning - A subset of machine learning that involves neural networks with many layers, enabling models to learn from large datasets.

Deep Q-Network (DQN) (Reinforcement Learning) - A model-free reinforcement learning algorithm combining Q-learning with deep learning.

Deepfake - AI-generated or altered media content (typically video or audio) designed to look and sound realistic.

Dimensionality Reduction - The process of reducing the number of features in a dataset while retaining its essential characteristics.

Dropout (Regularization in Neural Networks) - A technique to prevent overfitting by randomly dropping units from the neural network during training.

E

Edge AI - AI that processes data locally on devices rather than relying on cloud computing, reducing latency.

Embedding - A representation of data in a lower-dimensional space used in machine learning tasks such as NLP.

Embodied AI (Robotics, AI Systems) - AI systems that are

physically integrated into robots or devices, enabling interaction with the physical world.

End-to-End Learning (Neural Networks) - A learning approach where a system is trained directly on the input-output mapping without intermediate steps.

Ensemble Learning - A technique that combines multiple machine learning models to improve performance.

Epoch - A full iteration over the entire dataset during the training phase of a machine learning model.

Evolutionary Algorithm - Optimization algorithms inspired by the process of natural selection.

Exabyte (EB) - A data unit equivalent to 1,024 petabytes.

Expert System - An AI system that mimics the decision-making ability of a human expert.

Explainable AI (XAI) - AI systems designed to provide human-understandable explanations for their decisions and outputs.

F

Feature Engineering - The process of selecting, modifying, and creating features for improving machine learning models.

Feature Extraction - The process of transforming raw data into a set of features to be used by a machine learning model.

Federated Learning - A technique where models are trained across multiple devices without sharing raw data, improving privacy.

Few-Shot Learning - A type of machine learning where a model is trained with very few labeled examples.

Fine-tuning - Adjusting the parameters of a pre-trained model to apply it to a specific task.

Firmware - A specialized type of software that is embedded directly into hardware devices to control their functions. Firmware is typically stored in non-volatile memory and manages the basic operations of hardware, including devices used in AI systems, such as sensors and robotics.

Flask - A lightweight Python web application framework.

279

Fuzzy Logic - A form of logic used in AI that allows reasoning with uncertain or approximate values, rather than precise ones.

G

Generative AI - AI systems capable of generating new data, such as images, text, or music, that resemble human-created content.

Generative Adversarial Network (GAN) - A model consisting of two networks, a generator and a discriminator, that learn together to generate realistic data.

Genetic Algorithm - An optimization algorithm based on principles of natural selection and genetics.

Gigabyte (GB) - A unit of data equivalent to 1,024 megabytes.

Gradient Clipping (Optimization in Deep Learning) - A technique used to prevent exploding gradients during the training of neural networks.

Gradient Descent - An optimization algorithm used to minimize a loss function by iteratively moving in the direction of the steepest descent.

Graph Neural Network - A type of neural network that directly operates on graph structures, enabling learning on data that is structured as graphs.

Graphics Processing Unit (GPU) - A specialized processor designed for parallel processing tasks, originally used for rendering graphics. In AI, GPUs are widely used for training deep learning models due to their ability to handle multiple computations simultaneously, significantly speeding up the training process.

H

HTML (Hypertext Markup Language) - The standard markup language for creating web pages and web applications.

Hallucination (in AI) - When an AI model generates output (such as a response or image) that is factually incorrect or

AI TOOLBOX: EMPOWERING THE LEARNER

nonsensical.

Hardware - The physical components of a computer or device that perform computational tasks. In AI, hardware includes processors (like CPUs, GPUs, TPUs), storage, sensors, and other equipment that provides the computational power needed to train models and execute AI algorithms.

Heuristic - A problem-solving approach that uses practical methods or rules of thumb for making decisions.

Hybrid AI - Systems combining symbolic reasoning and neural networks to leverage the strengths of both approaches.

Hyperparameter - Parameters in machine learning models that are set before training and not learned from the data.

Hyperparameter Tuning - The process of adjusting hyperparameters to optimize the performance of a machine learning model.

I

Imbalanced Dataset - A dataset where some classes are significantly over- or under-represented, which can affect model performance.

Inference - The process of making predictions using a trained machine learning model.

Interpretable Machine Learning (IML) - Techniques that enable understanding and explaining how machine learning models make decisions.

J

JavaScript - A high-level, interpreted programming language that is a core technology of the World Wide Web.

K

K-Means Clustering - A clustering algorithm that partitions data into K distinct groups based on similarity.

K-Nearest Neighbors (KNN) - A machine learning algorithm that classifies data points based on the closest

281

labeled examples in the dataset.

Kernel Method - Techniques in machine learning that use a kernel function to enable algorithms to operate in a high-dimensional space.

Kilobyte (KB) - A data unit equivalent to 1,024 bytes.

Knowledge Base - A structured database of information used to support AI systems, such as expert systems.

Knowledge Distillation - A technique in which a smaller model is trained to replicate the behavior of a larger, more complex model.

L

Large Language Model (LLM) - A deep learning model trained on vast amounts of text data to understand and generate human-like text.

Learning Rate (Gradient Descent) - A hyperparameter that determines the step size for updating weights in gradient-based optimization.

Long Short-Term Memory (LSTM) - A type of recurrent neural network capable of learning long-term dependencies in sequential data.

Loss Function (Optimization) - A function used to measure the error or difference between the predicted output of a model and the actual outcome.

M

Machine Learning (ML) - A subset of AI that involves systems learning patterns from data and improving over time without being explicitly programmed.

Machine Learning Operations (MLOps) - A set of practices for deploying, managing, and monitoring machine learning models in production.

Markov Decision Process (MDP) (Reinforcement Learning) - A framework for modeling decision-making where outcomes are partly random and partly under the control of an agent.

Megabyte (MB) - A data unit equivalent to 1,024 kilobytes.

Meta-Learning - A machine learning approach where models learn how to learn, improving their adaptability to new tasks.

Model - A mathematical representation of a system, process, or behavior that can make predictions or decisions based on input data.

Model Compression - Techniques to reduce the size and complexity of machine learning models while maintaining performance.

Monte Carlo Method (Statistical Learning) - A computational algorithm that uses random sampling to solve problems that might be deterministic in principle.

Multi-Agent System - A system composed of multiple interacting intelligent agents that work together or compete to achieve goals.

Multi-Task Learning - A machine learning approach where a model is trained on multiple related tasks simultaneously, sharing knowledge across tasks.

MySQL - An open-source relational database management system that uses Structured Query Language (SQL).

N

Natural Language Generation (NLG) - The use of AI to generate human-like language based on structured data or inputs.

Natural Language Processing (NLP) - A field of AI that focuses on the interaction between computers and human language.

Natural Language Understanding (NLU) - A subfield of NLP focused on understanding the meaning and context of human language.

Neural Architecture Search - The process of automating the design of neural network architectures using machine learning.

Neural Tangent Kernel (Theoretical ML) - A theoretical

framework for understanding the behavior of neural networks during training.

Neurosymbolic AI - An approach combining neural networks and symbolic reasoning to enhance the interpretability of AI systems.

Node.js - An open-source, cross-platform JavaScript runtime environment that executes JavaScript code outside of a web browser.

Noisy Student (Data Augmentation) - A technique that improves the accuracy of models by training them on both labeled and noisy augmented data.

O

One-Shot Learning - A form of learning where a model can recognize new objects or patterns after being trained on a single example.

Ontology - A structured representation of knowledge and concepts used in AI for reasoning about relationships and entities.

Open Source - Software or models made available with a license that allows anyone to view, modify, and distribute the source code. Open-source AI tools are often free to use, though they may have associated costs for implementation or support. These tools promote collaboration and transparency in the development of AI technologies.

Optimizer (Deep Learning) - Algorithms or methods used to minimize the loss function and improve the accuracy of a model during training.

Overfitting - A scenario where a machine learning model learns too closely from training data, performing poorly on unseen data.

P

PHP - A server-side scripting language designed for web development.

Parameter - Variables in a machine learning model that are

learned from data during training, such as weights in a neural network.

Pattern Recognition - The ability of AI models to recognize patterns or regularities in data.

Perceptron - The simplest type of artificial neural network, primarily used in binary classification tasks.

Permutation Importance - A technique for measuring the importance of features in a machine learning model by evaluating the change in model performance after shuffling each feature.

Petabyte (PB) - A unit of data equal to 1,024 terabytes.

Predictive Analytics - Using statistical techniques and machine learning to predict future outcomes based on historical data.

Preprocessing - Preparing and transforming raw data into a suitable format for training machine learning models.

Proprietary - Software, models, or systems that are owned by a company or individual and have restrictions on access, usage, and modification. Proprietary AI tools may require a license or payment to use and are typically closed to public modification and distribution. Access is often limited based on a pay-to-use model, though some proprietary tools may offer free tiers with limited functionality.

Pruning - A technique to reduce the size of a neural network by eliminating weights or neurons that contribute little to model accuracy.

Python - A high-level, interpreted programming language known for its simplicity and readability, widely used in AI, data science, and web development.

Q

Quantum Computing - A type of computing that leverages quantum mechanics to perform calculations at exponentially faster rates than classical computers.

R

Random Forest (Ensemble Learning) - An ensemble learning technique that uses multiple decision trees to improve prediction accuracy.

React - A JavaScript library for building user interfaces, particularly single-page applications.

Recurrent Neural Network (RNN) - A type of neural network designed to handle sequential data such as time series or text.

Regression - A type of supervised learning used to predict continuous outcomes based on input features.

Regularization (Preventing Overfitting) - Techniques used to reduce overfitting by adding constraints to a machine learning model.

Reinforcement Learning - A machine learning paradigm where agents learn to make decisions through rewards and punishments.

Robotics - The use of AI in designing and building machines that can perform tasks typically carried out by humans.

Rule-Based System - AI systems that apply a set of predefined rules to reach conclusions or make decisions.

S

SQL (Structured Query Language) - A standardized language used for managing and manipulating relational databases.

Self-Supervised Learning (Machine Learning) - A learning approach where models learn from unlabeled data by creating their own labels.

Semantic Analysis - The process of understanding the meaning and context of language in AI and NLP tasks.

Sentiment Analysis - An NLP technique used to determine the sentiment (positive, negative, neutral) expressed in text.

Software - Programs and applications that run on hardware to perform specific tasks. In AI, software refers to the code, frameworks, and models that enable data processing, model training, and decision-making. AI software can be proprietary or open-source and may operate on various types of hardware.

Sparsity (ML models) - A concept in machine learning where only a small percentage of features are relevant to the model's output.

Supervised Learning - A type of machine learning where the model is trained on labeled data, learning to predict output based on input features.

Support Vector Machine (SVM) - A supervised learning algorithm used for classification and regression tasks by finding the hyperplane that best separates data points.

Swarm Intelligence (Multi-Agent Systems) - A collective behavior of decentralized, self-organized agents used in AI to solve complex problems.

Synthetic Data - Artificially generated data used to train AI models, often used when real-world data is scarce or sensitive.

T

Tensor Processing Unit (TPU) - A specialized hardware accelerator designed by Google specifically for AI and machine learning tasks, particularly for deep learning and neural networks. TPUs are optimized for TensorFlow workloads and offer faster computation than CPUs and GPUs for specific AI tasks, especially in large-scale training.

Terabyte (TB) - A unit of data storage equal to 1,024 gigabytes.

Tokenization (NLP) - The process of breaking text into smaller units, such as words or subwords, for analysis in NLP models.

Transfer Learning - A technique where a pre-trained model is adapted to perform a new, but related, task.

Transformer - A deep learning architecture designed for tasks such as NLP that relies on attention mechanisms to process input data.

Turing Test - A test proposed by Alan Turing to evaluate

a machine's ability to exhibit intelligent behavior indistinguishable from that of a human.

U

UX - Short for User Experience, refers to the design and interaction of users with a product or service, especially important in AI system interfaces.

Unsupervised Learning - A machine learning paradigm where models are trained on unlabeled data to find patterns or structure.

V

Validation Set - A subset of the data used to tune model parameters and avoid overfitting during the training process.

Vector - A mathematical representation of data points in machine learning and deep learning.

Virtual Reality (VR) - The use of computer technology to create simulated, immersive environments.

Voice Recognition - AI technology that identifies and processes human speech for various applications.

W

WordPress - An open-source content management system based on PHP and MySQL.

X

XML (eXtensible Markup Language) - A markup language that defines a set of rules for encoding documents in a format that is both human-readable and machine-readable.

Y

Yottabyte (YB) - The largest standard unit of data storage, equivalent to 1,024 zettabytes.

Z

Zero-Shot Learning (Machine Learning) - A learning approach where the model makes predictions on classes or tasks it has not been explicitly trained on.

Zettabyte (ZB) - A data unit equivalent to 1,024 exabytes.

ABOUT NEWBITS.AI

The newbits.ai ecosystem emerged from a simple yet powerful vision: to demystify artificial intelligence and make this complex technological frontier accessible to everyone. This dynamic learning environment, where learning, discovery, and innovation flourish together, was created by an AI enthusiast and curator, who authored the *NewBits AI Trilogy*: *AI Basics: The Fundamentals*, *AI Toolbox: Empowering the Learner*, and *AI Frontier: Navigating the Cutting Edge*. This digital nexus, accessible through the internet domain newbits.ai, mirrors the books' mission to bridge the gap between cutting edge AI technology and curious minds at all levels.

At the foundation of newbits.ai stands the *AI Solutions* Marketplace, a carefully curated space where theory meets practical application. Here, visitors discover a rich tapestry of artificial intelligence tools spanning six essential categories: Language, Data, Audio/Vision, Healthcare, Robotics, and Gaming. Within Language, users find natural language processing tools and translation systems. The Data category offers analytics platforms and data management solutions.

Audio/Vision presents solutions for speech recognition, image processing, computer vision, and visualization tools. Healthcare showcases medical imaging and diagnostic innovations. Robotics features autonomous systems and control software, while Gaming presents AI driven development tools and virtual reality platforms.

The marketplace distinguishes between models and tools and platforms, allowing users to focus their search based on their specific needs. Visitors can easily navigate between open source and proprietary solutions, ensuring they find resources that align with their preferences and requirements. Through intuitive browsing and filtering options, users can refine their search by category, solution type, and featured solutions, transforming what could be an overwhelming journey into a streamlined discovery process.

Each listing offers detailed insights and community reviews, ensuring that whether someone is taking their first steps into AI implementation or seeking advanced platforms for complex projects, they can make informed decisions with confidence.

Beyond the marketplace lies the *AI Hub*, a vibrant community space that pulses with the energy of shared discovery. This dynamic network spans across nine distinct platforms: Reddit, YouTube, Spotify, Facebook, X (formerly Twitter), LinkedIn, Medium, Quora, and Discord. Through thoughtful discussions on Reddit, engaging content on YouTube and Spotify, industry insights on LinkedIn, enriching articles on Medium, knowledge sharing on Quora, community building on Facebook, and real time exchanges on Discord and X, the Hub weaves together a tapestry of knowledge where every voice contributes to our collective understanding. Here, beginners find mentorship, experts share insights, and innovations spark from the collision of curious minds.

The *AI Ed* page serves as the gateway to our signature educational content, featuring the podcast series *AI Ed: From*

Bits to Breakthroughs. Here, visitors can access a carefully structured journey that mirrors the natural progression of learning found in our book trilogy. The series begins with foundational concepts in *AI Basics: The Fundamentals*, advances through practical applications in *AI Toolbox: Empowering the Learner*, and ultimately explores the cutting edge of possibility in *AI Frontier: Navigating the Cutting Edge.* Each episode builds upon the last, creating a comprehensive narrative that guides listeners from their first encounter with artificial intelligence through to the most advanced concepts shaping our future.

Supporting this educational journey, the *AI Glossary: Bit by Bit* serves as a trusted companion, illuminating the path from basic terminology to complex concepts. This carefully crafted resource grows alongside our community, ensuring that the language of artificial intelligence remains accessible to all who wish to learn.

Together, these elements form something greater than their individual parts, standing as a testament to the power of accessible education, community collaboration, and practical implementation. Just as the book trilogy illuminates the path from fundamental concepts to cutting edge innovations, newbits.ai represents an unwavering commitment to transforming the complex world of artificial intelligence into a journey of discovery that anyone can undertake. As artificial intelligence continues to reshape our world, this commitment ensures that everyone has the opportunity to understand, implement, and innovate in this revolutionary field.

In the end, newbits.ai embodies a simple truth: that the future of artificial intelligence belongs not to a select few, but to everyone who dares to learn, to explore, and to imagine. Through educational content, community engagement, and comprehensive resources, the mission of demystifying AI continues, making the complex simple and the cutting edge accessible. After all, in this rapidly evolving landscape, every bit of knowledge counts, but none more so than the new bits that light the way forward.

OUR NAME: NEWBITS.AI

Names tell stories. They carry meaning, purpose, and vision. In the realm of artificial intelligence, where complex concepts meet practical applications, a name must bridge the gap between technical precision and accessible understanding. The story of newbits.ai begins with this bridge, connecting the foundational elements of digital technology with the transformative potential of human learning.

At the heart of every digital innovation lies a fundamental unit of information: the bit. This binary digit, capable of being either zero or one, forms the foundation of our name and reflects our mission in the world of artificial intelligence. To understand newbits.ai is to understand how the smallest unit of digital information scales to enable the vast possibilities of modern computing and artificial intelligence.

A bit, in its simplest form, acts like a tiny switch, either off or on. When eight bits come together, they form a byte, capable of representing a single character like a letter or number. As bits and bytes combine, they create progressively larger units that power the digital world we interact with every day:

Unit	Approximate Value	Real-World Example
Bit	Single binary value (0 or 1)	The smallest piece of data in computing
Byte	8 bits	A single character (e.g. 'A' or '5')
Kilobyte	1,024 bytes	A text document, simple email, or basic app
Megabyte	1,024 kilobytes	A high-resolution photo, MP3 song, or standard mobile app
Gigabyte	1,024 megabytes	A movie, complex app, or smartphone storage capacity
Terabyte	1,024 gigabytes	External hard drive, large data backups, or server storage
Petabyte	1,024 terabytes	Data centers, cloud storage providers, or large-scale AI datasets
Exabyte	1,024 petabytes	Total data generated globally in a year
Zettabyte	1,024 exabytes	Global data storage capacity
Yottabyte	1,024 zettabytes	Theoretical future data scale

In daily life, these units manifest in familiar ways. A simple text file or short email might occupy a few kilobytes. A high-quality photo, MP3 song, or standard mobile app typically requires several megabytes. Movies, complex applications, and smartphone storage capacities are measured in gigabytes. Large storage devices like external hard drives often hold terabytes of data. Data centers and major cloud providers work with petabytes, while units like exabytes, zettabytes, and yottabytes represent the immense scale of global data storage and future possibilities.

In terms of data transmission, these units determine the speed at which information travels across networks, measured in bits per second (bps). Internet speeds, typically measured in megabits per second, reflect how quickly data can be downloaded or uploaded, directly affecting everything from streaming videos to downloading applications.

The name newbits.ai carries this symbolism in each of its elements. "New" represents the constant evolution and innovation in artificial intelligence, acknowledging that yesterday's cutting edge becomes tomorrow's foundation. "Bits" holds dual significance, representing both the fundamental units of digital information and the incremental pieces of knowledge that accumulate to create understanding. The ".ai" domain extension definitively anchors our identity in artificial intelligence, declaring our dedicated focus on this transformative field.

Just as bits scale from simple binary values to the massive datasets that power modern artificial intelligence, newbits.ai scales from fundamental concepts to advanced applications. Through the *AI Solutions* Marketplace, each tool and platform represents countless bits working in harmony. In the *AI Hub*, every shared insight adds new bits of knowledge to our collective understanding. The *AI Ed* podcast series and *AI Glossary* transform complex concepts into accessible bits of learning, while this book trilogy guides readers through their journey from basic bits to breakthrough insights.

This scalability of bits, from foundational elements to complex systems, embodies the accessibility championed by newbits.ai. The phrase coined by the author, "It's all about the bits, especially the new bits," echoes through every aspect of artificial intelligence, celebrating both the technical foundation of digital innovation and the journey of continuous learning that defines the AI frontier. Each new bit of knowledge, like each binary digit in a computer system, builds upon what came before, creating ever greater possibilities for understanding, innovation, and discovery.

From the smallest bit to the largest dataset, from the first step into artificial intelligence to mastery of advanced concepts, the name newbits.ai captures the essence of digital evolution and perpetual learning in this revolutionary field.

EXTENDED DEDICATIONS

I dedicate this book to my parents, Frieda and Yair "Jerry" Oren, and to my wife Melissa's parents, Sharon and Jerry "Dr. J." Goodwin.

Mom and Dad, you gave me the gift of life, but more importantly, you enriched it beyond measure. Despite countless stories from family and friends about my challenging childhood, I have always felt your unwavering love and support. From as far back as I can remember, you provided a foundation of stability and warmth that shaped who I am today.

I was fortunate to witness how you prioritized our family in the United States while maintaining close ties with our extended family abroad and your many friends around the world. You surrounded my brothers, my older brother, Aeyal, and my younger brother, Matty, and me with love, friendship, and a strong sense of community.

Through our frequent travels, I had the privilege of meeting diverse people, experiencing various cultures, tasting intriguing foods, and learning the importance of appreciating

299

the world's richness. You taught me the value of family, both by blood and by choice, and thanks to this lesson, I cherish the time spent with loved ones.

Melissa, our children, Zachary, Sydney, and Ava, and I are always welcomed in your home. Dad, you eagerly engage with us, whether on the golf course or in the kitchen creating exceptional meals. Mom, you continually shower us with love, appreciation, and kindness. We are truly blessed to have you both in our lives.

Sharon and Jerry "Dr. J," you are more than Melissa's parents; you are incredible additions to our family. Marrying Melissa brought the precious gift of having you as my chosen family.

You embraced me with open arms and have consistently offered unwavering support, wisdom, and love, profoundly impacting our lives. Our children have special relationships with each of you, whether spending quality time in Miami or exploring the mountains of upstate New York.

Sharon, you set the standard for hospitality. Your home is always welcoming, beautifully decorated to reflect the season, and filled with the aromas of your unique culinary creations. Your legendary Thanksgiving feasts and magical Christmas celebrations are just glimpses of how you've woven love and tradition into the fabric of our family. We are truly blessed to have you in our lives.

Dr. J, you possess a unique ability to carry yourself with grace and humility while imparting positivity and wisdom to everyone around you. The lessons you've taught us are countless, but a few stand out: the gift of reading, the importance of purpose, balancing work and play, teaching our children life skills like golf, and demonstrating proper decorum through both words and actions. You are a precious gift to us all.

I am profoundly grateful for these four individuals whose wisdom, love, support, and guidance have shaped our family's journey and inspired generations. Thank you.

ABOUT THE AUTHOR

Gil Oren is a business strategist, critical thinker, and serial entrepreneur whose fascination with artificial intelligence inspired the *NewBits AI Trilogy*. With over two decades of experience tackling complex business challenges, he offers unique insights into understanding and applying AI technology.

His multidisciplinary expertise spans law, real estate development, private equity, intellectual property, research and development, manufacturing, marketing, distribution, sales, and sustainability. This diverse background enables him to relate AI concepts effectively across various industries.

For over 15 years, Gil led an organization in the chemical industry operating in institutional, industrial, commercial, consumer, and infrastructure markets across the Americas, Europe, Australia, the Middle East, and Asia. Collaborating with startups, Fortune 100 companies, nation-states, and armed forces, he gained deep insights into global business and technology implementation.

An innovator at heart, he developed award-winning proprietary technologies and received patents worldwide. By designing training procedures for these novel technologies, he demonstrated his capacity for practical application of complex ideas, offering firsthand insights into adopting transformative technologies like AI.

As an accomplished speaker and advocate for sustainable technologies, Gil has appeared on Fox News, NPR, the Discovery Channel, and QVC, promoting innovative solutions. His ability to communicate complex ideas to diverse audiences underscores his dedication to making transformative technologies accessible.

Serving as an Executive Chairman, Board Member, and licensed attorney in the State of Florida and the District of Columbia, Gil brings profound understanding of strategic technology implementation, governance, and regulatory aspects of technology adoption. This combination strengthens his ability to guide readers through the complexities of AI integration in business.

Driven by a mission to empower individuals and organizations, Gil focuses on demystifying AI tools, enabling readers to confidently apply AI concepts in real-world scenarios. In *AI Toolbox: Empowering the Learner*, the second installment of the *NewBits AI Trilogy*, he builds upon the fundamentals from his first book, providing actionable tools and techniques to navigate the AI landscape effectively.

When not exploring artificial intelligence and emerging technologies, Gil enjoys spending time with family and friends, playing piano and guitar, and following collegiate and professional sports.

He firmly believes that relationships and teamwork are fundamental to achieving success in life and in business.